USA TODAY

Lifeline

BIOGRAPHIES

◼◼◻◻

BARACK OBAMA

A Leader in a Time of Change

by Karen Sirvaitis

Twenty-First Century Books · Minneapolis

Twenty-First Century Books
A division of Lerner Publishing Group, Inc.
241 First Avenue North
Minneapolis, MN 55401 U.S.A.

Website address: www.lernerbooks.com

The publisher wishes to thank Phil Pruitt and Ben Nussbaum of USA TODAY for their help in preparing this book.

Library of Congress Cataloging-in-Publication Data

Sirvaitis, Karen, 1961–
    Barack Obama : a leader in a time of change / by Karen Sirvaitis.
        p.   cm. — (USA TODAY lifeline biographies)
    Includes bibliographical references and index.
    ISBN 978–0–7613–4235–9 (lib. bdg. : alk. paper)
    1. Obama, Barack—Juvenile literature. 2. Presidents—United States—Biography—Juvenile literature. 3. Racially mixed people—United States—Biography—Juvenile literature. I. Title.
    E901.1.O23S577 2010
    973.932092—dc22 [B]   2009003097

Manufactured in the United States of America
1 2 3 4 5 6 – PA – 15 14 13 12 11 10

USA TODAY Lifeline BIOGRAPHIES

Seizing the moment: Barack Obama gives the keynote address at the Democratic National Convention in Boston, Massachusetts, in 2004. The speech introduced the Illinois state senator to many Americans.

Common Ground

"I think he could be our first black president." remarked a woman at the 2004 Democratic National Convention (DNC) in Boston, Massachusetts. The woman had just heard an exciting speech from the convention floor. The whole crowd attending it was excited, revved up. Some people were crying, and most others were cheering wildly. Many were doing both. The audience and the media kept repeating that it was the best speech ever given at a political convention.

The speaker was Barack Obama, a little-known state senator from Illinois. He was there to support John Kerry, the 2004 Democratic presidential nominee. Kerry had invited Obama to be the keynote speaker. He had been impressed with the young senator, who was smart and likable.

Barack Obama was also campaigning for himself that year. He was running for the office of U.S. senator from Illinois. On Election Day, four months after the convention, John Kerry lost, but Barack Obama won the seat representing Illinois in the U.S. Senate. A mere four years later, Obama was still in Washington, but he was doing more than representing Illinois. He was representing the entire United States of America.

On November 4, 2008, Americans elected Barack Obama president of the United States. He is the first African American ever elected to

Making history: Barack Obama is sworn in as president by Chief Justice John Roberts on January 20, 2009. Obama's wife, Michelle, holds the Bible. His daughters, Malia and Natasha *(front, far right)*, watch the ceremony.

New president: President Obama deals with many complex responsibilities as the forty-fourth president of the United States.

serve as U.S. president. This achievement, 143 years after the end of slavery in the United States, happened in a country divided politically and racially. Barack Obama won the hearts and trust of millions of Americans and encouraged a near-record number of voters to go to the polls. Here's the story of

USA TODAY Snapshots®

'O' to be president!

Barack Obama will be the first president whose last name starts with an O, leaving D, I, Q, S, U, X, Y and Z still unelected.

Most common presidential initial

H

Harding
Benjamin Harrison
William H. Harrison
Hayes
Hoover

Source:
www.biography.com

By Anne R. Carey and Suzy Parker, USA TODAY, 2009

how one man persuaded millions of Americans to look beyond their differences and to see what they have in common.

CHAPTER ONE

Barack Obama Sr.: Barack's father was from Kenya, a nation on the east coast of Africa.

Across Oceans and Continents

Barack Hussein Obama was born August 4, 1961, in Honolulu, Hawaii. Barack is an Arabic and Swahili name that means "blessed." The name was given to him by his father, Barack Obama Sr., a black African from a small village in Kenya. Barack Sr. had only two sisters, but he had a large extended family. His father, Hussein Onyango Obama, was very strict. His mother, Akumu, left the family when Barack Sr. was still a boy.

Barack's mother came from a very different background. Ann Dunham was a white woman who grew up in the state of Kansas. An only child, she and her parents moved a lot. Ann finished high school in Washington State, and then the family moved to Hawaii. Her parents, Stanley and Madelyn Dunham, opened a furniture store.

Stanley Ann: Barack's mother, Stanley Ann Dunham, grew up in Kansas. She attended high school on Mercer Island, Washington. This sophomore year photo from her yearbook is signed, "To 'Max' from your pal, Stanley."

Barack's parents met while students at the University of Hawaii. Barack Sr. (known as Barry) was the university's first African student. He had received a full scholarship

Ann Dunham's name is actually Stanley Ann Dunham. Her parents were expecting their first child to be a boy. When Ann was born, Stanley and Madelyn kept the name they had already picked out. Ann later officially dropped her first name and instead used her middle name.

to study economics. Ann was studying to be an anthropologist (someone who studies humans and their cultures). When Ann introduced Barack to her parents, Stanley and Madelyn welcomed him. They appreciated his intelligence and sense of humor. When the couple announced their engagement a short time later, Ann's parents were a little less sure about the relationship. Mixed-race couples were not common during the 1960s. But they accepted their daughter's choice.

Onyango Obama, Barack's father, was even less sure. He told his son that he thought that Ann would not be willing to follow the customs of the Luo people (the Obamas' ethnic group) because her culture was too different. Regardless of what others thought, the couple married in 1960.

IN FOCUS

The Luo of Kenya

Barack Obama Sr. was a member of the Luo. This African ethnic group includes more than three million people. The Luo live in several African nations, including Kenya, Uganda, and Tanzania. They are the third-largest ethnic group in Kenya, after the Kikuyu and the Luhya.

When Barack Obama Sr. went to the United States in the late 1950s, Kenya was a British colony. Because the English-speaking British ruled Kenya, children there learned to speak English in school. They also learned Swahili (a language spoken throughout much of East Africa). At home they learned their tribal language.

Shortly after Barack Jr. was born in Hawaii, Kenya gained its independence from Great Britain. A Luo leader, Oginga Odinga, declined the presidency and became independent Kenya's first vice president. He led the country alongside President Jomo Kenyatta, a Kikuyu.

IN FOCUS

The 1960s

Barack Obama was born during a time when his parents' marriage was illegal in nineteen states. Many people believed it was wrong for whites to marry blacks. Some states had enacted Jim Crow laws, or laws discriminating against African Americans and requiring blacks and whites to use separate facilities. Blacks could ride the same bus as whites, but they had to sit in the back. Black children went to separate public schools. Blacks could serve in the military, as long as they stayed in separate units in separate barracks. Other public places such as restaurants and restrooms were also kept separate.

In the early 1960s, some southern states still enforced Jim Crow laws. Hawaii, a relatively new state, did not have such laws or even many black residents. But in the mainland United States, as people protested against U.S. involvement in a war in Vietnam, they also protested against discrimination toward African Americans and other minorities. Sometimes the protests were peaceful, but at times, they ended in violence.

The decade was a time when the people in the United States were forced to question their beliefs about skin color, gender, and equal rights. The 1960s introduced a period of change. While it would take a long time for many old beliefs about race to fade, a new era focusing on racial equality had at least begun. It was into this climate that Barack Obama was born. Yet for the first years of his life, he had no idea that skin color was supposed to matter.

Jim Crow laws: Separate drinking fountains for blacks and whites were one form of Jim Crow discrimination. These laws were in effect from 1876 until the Supreme Court declared them unconstitutional in 1965.

Divorce

In 1963 the elder Obama left Hawaii to complete his studies at Harvard University in Cambridge, Massachusetts. The couple planned to live in Kenya when he finished school. Meanwhile, young Barack and his mother lived with her parents. To Barack, his grandparents were Gramps and Tutu (the Hawaiian name for "grandmother"), or Toot for short.

While separated, Ann and her husband had time to think about their relationship. Kenya had just achieved independence from Great Britain, and the government was unstable. Toot didn't want Ann to move to Africa. She was afraid for her daughter's and grandson's safety. The elder Obama thought about his loyalty to his father and his people. His family expected him to return to Kenya, to find a high-paying job, and to help his newly freed country. In 1964, when Barack was two, the couple divorced. Ann went back to the university after taking two years off to raise her son. In 1965, after getting a master's degree in economics from Harvard, Barack Obama Sr. returned to Kenya.

Young Barack was growing up without a father, but he was a happy and well-adjusted child. His mother and grandparents were devoted to him. And although they earned only a modest income, they gave Barack whatever they could.

Mother and son: Barack's parents divorced when he was two. He was raised by his mother *(shown with Barack in the early 1960s)* and his grandparents in Hawaii.

While at the University of Hawaii, Ann met and married Lolo Soetoro, a student from Indonesia. This Asian country is made up of about seventeen thousand islands. They decided to live in Indonesia. Soetoro returned to Indonesia ahead of Ann and Barack, who followed soon afterward. By this time, Barack was six years old.

Lucky Kid

Barack and his mother arrived in Jakarta, the capital city of Indonesia, on a hot day in 1967. Soetoro picked them up at the airport in a borrowed car. The family pulled up to the gate of a modest house made of stucco and with a red tile roof. Soetoro told Barack he had a surprise for him. "Before he could explain we heard a deafening howl from high up in the tree," Barack later wrote. "My mother and I jumped back with a start and saw a big, hairy creature with a small, flat head and long, menacing arms drop onto a low branch. 'A monkey!' I shouted. 'An ape,' my mother corrected."

A new country to call home: Barack explored Jakarta's busy streets with his mother and her new husband, Lolo.

Barack's stepfather explained that the ape's name was Tata. Tata was from the jungles of New Guinea, a large Southeast Asian island. Tata was Barack's new pet. But there were more. Chickens, ducks, exotic birds, and a dog ran around the backyard. Farther back, a small fenced-off pond contained two baby crocodiles. As Barack fell asleep that first night, he felt like one of the luckiest kids on Earth.

 When Barack lived in Indonesia, he learned to speak Bahasa Indonesia, the official language of Indonesia. Nearly 100 percent of the country's 240 million people speak the language. Most Indonesians are fluent in a regional language as well, such as Balinese (on the island of Bali) and Javanese (on the island of Java). Although Barack hasn't used the language of his youth very often, he still manages to speak passable Bahasa Indonesia.

"One Long Adventure"

Soon after arriving in his new homeland, Barack was involved in a fight with another kid over a stolen soccer ball. But for the most part, he fit into his new surroundings perfectly. Within six months, he could speak the language. He survived several childhood illnesses, including chicken pox and the measles. And he had a large group of friends to play with. Barack and his buddies ran the streets of Jakarta, catching crickets and flying kites.

Barack would later describe his time in Indonesia as "one long adventure." But in addition to all the fun and games, he witnessed the harsher side of life in Jakarta. Thousands of beggars and people with illnesses roamed the streets, unable to find work or to afford proper medical care. His stepfather helped Barack deal with his feelings about seeing such hardship. He told Barack it was not about good or bad. It was about accepting that life brings many different experiences, whether we like them or not. Soetoro helped Barack in other ways too. He taught the boy to box so he could defend himself in a fight.

Barack's mother appreciated the time and attention her husband gave to her son. Soetoro was a good father to him. She also liked the idea that Barack's world was one big playground. And she was grateful that he was able to experience how people live in a country so different from the United States. But she had concerns as well. She worried about her son's education, his safety, and about some of the values he was learning. It was not okay, for instance, for parents to bribe teachers with gifts to ensure their children got good grades. It was not okay to hide possessions so owners wouldn't be taxed on them, even if this was customary.

School in Indonesia: Barack *(back row, circled in yellow)* is pictured with his classmates at one of the schools he attended in Indonesia.

His mother tried to emphasize the importance of honesty, fairness, and independent thinking—values she learned growing up in Kansas. To help Barack keep up his studies in English, she enrolled her son in a U.S. correspondence course, where students receive lessons by mail. In addition, every morning at four o'clock, she awoke Barack to give him English lessons for three hours before he went to school and she went to work. Barack disliked these painfully early lessons, but his mother persisted. "This is no picnic for me either, buster," she would say.

 Barack grew up with different religious influences. His grandparents were nonpracticing Christians. His mother was agnostic, or doubtful that God existed. His father and stepfather were nonpracticing Muslims. His grandfather, Hussein Onyango Obama, was Muslim. In Indonesia, Barack attended a Muslim school and a Roman Catholic school. Religion did not mean too much to him until he was in his twenties and joined a Protestant Christian church.

A Lesson in *Life*

Barack's mother worked at the U.S. Embassy in Jakarta, teaching English to Indonesian businesspeople. One day, when Barack was nine years old, she took him to her office while she worked. He kept himself busy by looking through magazines. Eventually Barack picked up an issue of *Life*, a magazine known for its photography. Barack played a game of looking at a picture in the magazine and guessing what the article was about.

The story behind one image in particular eluded him. The picture was of a man wearing dark glasses and an overcoat, walking down an empty road. Barack turned the page and saw another photograph. This one showed the man's hands close up. They had a strange pale and ghostly color to them, "as if blood had been drawn from the flesh." This piqued Barack's interest, and he read the article. The man's discolored skin was the result of a chemical treatment he went through to try to whiten his complexion. The man was African American. The treatment had failed, leaving him scarred for life.

Barack's view of himself and the world changed that day. For the first time, he had realized that in the eyes of society, black people were somehow inferior.

 Some researchers have questioned Obama's story about the article in *Life* magazine, claiming that no one can find any record of the article in *Life* archives. Obama acknowledges in the book that he changed some names and other details. He realizes that memories of past events are not always 100 percent accurate.

A New Life

In August 1970, Barack's mother and Soetoro had their first child together, a girl they named Maya. The following summer, his mother sent Barack to Hawaii to live with her parents. Soon he would be ten years old and entering the fifth grade. His mother was concerned about the education he was getting in Indonesia. His grandfather was able to enroll Barack in a prestigious school in Honolulu. So in 1971, Barack returned to Hawaii to live with Gramps and Toot.

Family portrait: Barack *(far right)* was nine when this photo was taken of him with his stepfather, Lolo Soetoro; mother, Ann; and half sister Maya. Soon Barack would move back to Hawaii and live with his grandparents.

Barack hadn't seen Toot and Gramps in four years. He felt as though he were moving in with strangers at first, but soon he felt right at home. His grandfather had a job selling insurance. His grandmother was vice president of a local bank—the first woman in that branch to hold that position.

As fall approached, Barack and his grandparents prepared for the boy's entrance into Punahou Academy. Gramps, in particular, was proud of the fact that his grandson was enrolled there. Barack was just glad to have a chance to make some friends.

Barack's troubles started the moment his teacher called his name in front of the class. Barack had been calling himself Barry, the name his father had adopted as a student at the University of Hawaii. The name Barry was familiar to Americans. When his new teacher said "Barack," classmates started to giggle. Things only got worse when the teacher started to talk about Kenya. She knew Barack's father was Kenyan, and she had spent time there herself. When she asked what tribe his father was from, the class could no longer contain their laughter.

At one time or another in history, all races of people lived in tribes, or family groups. European, Native American, African, Asian, and other peoples grouped their families together for many reasons. These small ethnic groups provide safety and help to ensure that people's basic needs are met. These groups also give people a strong sense of belonging.

Having dark skin and an African name set Barack apart from the other students at Punahou, most of whom were either white or Asian. To help himself fit in, Barack told some kids that his father was a prince and that the name Obama meant "burning spear." This gained him some prestige—for a while at least. But he continued to endure some teasing and rude behavior from his classmates. It helped him accept it when he realized that other kids felt like misfits too.

Back to Hawaii: Barack *(back row, third from left)*, is shown here with his fifth-grade class at Punahou Academy in Hawaii.

A Visit from Dad

A few months into the school year, Barack's grandmother received a telegram. Barack's father was coming to visit. He planned to stay with the family for an entire month while he recovered from an injury he had received in an automobile accident. Ann and Maya would also return from Indonesia for an extended stay. Barack didn't have any memories of his father—only stories and pictures to help shape an image of him. His mother told him that his father had a new wife and that Barack had five brothers and one sister in Kenya. With so little information to go on, the boy really didn't know what to expect.

The elder Barack Obama proved to be friendly. Every evening the family would joke and laugh and tell stories. But he was also rather strict.

Father and son: Barack's father visited the family in Hawaii once, in 1972. Barack was ten years old.

One night, when Barack wanted to see a Christmas special on television, his father sent him to his room to study, saying he watched too much TV. His father expected Barack to commit himself to his studies, as he had. Gramps and Toot didn't appreciate the elder Obama interfering. Then his mother criticized her parents for getting involved. The small family argument left Barack feeling uneasy. At that point, he wanted only for his father to leave so that everything could return to normal.

Then it happened. His mom casually informed him that his teacher wanted his father to talk to the fifth-grade class about Kenya. A sense of dread filled Barack as he thought about his own stories of princes and burning spears. He also remembered the first day of class. One mention of the word *tribe*, and Barack would never hear the end of it.

A Surprise Ending

Barack noticed that his father seemed to have a "strange power." During family conversations, he would be able to get all the adults to participate. He had a deep voice with a British accent. When he spoke, he got people's attention.

Barack's classmates seemed to feel the power as well. When the elder Obama started to tell stories about Kenya, the students were captivated. He talked about Kenya's land and wildlife. He talked about traditions and how the Masai people of Kenya required boys to kill a lion to prove their manhood. He talked about respect for elders and Kenya's struggle to be free from British rule. He spoke with confidence, and he made good sense. His presence seemed to comfort

Kenyan culture: Barack Obama Sr. talked to Barack's class about people in Kenya, including the Masai. Here Masai warriors are covered in white clay while participating in a ceremony to become junior elders.

people. Afterward, Barack's classmates asked questions. Luckily, no one asked about his princely duties. Instead, they came up to Barack to tell him how cool they thought his dad was. Two weeks later, his father returned to Kenya, and his mother and sister left for Indonesia.

Another Separation

In 1973 Ann and Maya came back to Hawaii, and the three of them moved into a small apartment close to Punahou Academy. His mother spent the next three years working on a master's degree in anthropology at the University of Hawaii. When her studies were finished, she was ready to return to Indonesia to do fieldwork—further studies away from the university. She wanted her children to return with her, but Barack refused. He was about to start high school at Punahou. He had friends and a life. The last thing he wanted was to have to start over again in a new school. So they agreed that his mother and sister would return to Indonesia. Barack would stay with Gramps and Toot.

USA TODAY Snapshots®

Presidential roots

Barack Obama, born in Hawaii, is one of seven presidents born west of the Mississippi River. States where more than one president were born:

Massachusetts **4**

Vermont **2**

New York **4**

Ohio **7**

Virginia **8**

2

North Carolina

Texas **2**

Source: National Geographic

By Anne R. Carey and Web Bryant, USA TODAY, 2009

High School

Barack and his father had exchanged letters over the years. The elder Obama would tell Barack about his family in Kenya, and Barack would tell his dad how he was doing in school. But eventually the letters stopped. As a tenth grader, Barack had begun to question who and what he was. Like most teenagers, he was experimenting with what kind of person he wanted to be—how he would treat others and how he wanted others to view him. Unlike most teenagers, he not only had to decide what kind of person he wanted to be, but he also needed to figure out how race fit into his life. Biologically he was black and white. Because his skin was dark, he had felt the sting of discrimination from white people. But the people who raised him—the people he loved most—were white.

Barack's mother and grandparents were careful to treat all people with respect and fairness. They understood that discrimination was hurtful. But Barack knew they could never completely understand how it felt. And while he knew what discrimination felt like, he didn't truly know what it meant to be a black man. His only role model lived thousands of miles away. He wasn't any help. And so by the time he reached the tenth grade, Barack had stopped writing to his father.

Senior year: This photo is from Obama's senior yearbook at Punahou Academy.

The Need to Belong

Barack spent his high school years seeking to belong to a black community. He read books by black authors such as James Ellison and Langston Hughes. He went to parties given by local African Americans and began to distrust whites who appeared to want to get along with blacks too eagerly. He found a community of black people who welcomed him on the basketball court in the local playground. He began to play basketball with a passion, and he made Punahou's basketball team. Still, Barack later wrote, he was going through a "fitful interior struggle. I was trying to raise myself to be a black man in America,

For the love of basketball: Obama, wearing number 23, goes up for a shot during a high school basketball game.

and beyond the given of my appearance, no one around me seemed to know exactly what that meant."

He asked himself what it meant to be black in the United States. Did it mean he deserved to be treated with less respect than white people? Did it mean he was supposed to mistrust white people? None of those ideas felt right to Barack. Why should he be treated differently? And why should he talk poorly about white people in general, when that included his mother, Gramps, and Toot? Barack had plenty of friends and family. But by the time he graduated from high school, he wrote that he felt, "utterly alone."

CHAPTER TWO

The graduate: Obama's grandmother Madelyn Dunham hugs him during his high school graduation ceremony. His grandfather Stanley Dunham is pictured at right.

Getting an Education

■■■■

After graduating from high school in 1979, Obama was ready to start college. He didn't have a major in mind but chose to attend Occidental College, a small liberal arts school in Los Angeles, California. He was ready for a change and anxious to get away from his life in Hawaii. In August he packed his bags and headed for the mainland.

While in Los Angeles, Obama enrolled in many of the courses that are required to get a college degree. He studied a little and went to classes. He hung out with newfound friends, enjoyed a bit of big city life, and became a little involved in politics. About this time, Obama's mother and Lolo Soetoro divorced. Ann and Maya, however, stayed in Indonesia. Obama wrote to his father again and received a letter in return. His father encouraged him to come to Kenya to meet his family. His father also told him he could stay as long as he wanted. A visit to his ancestral homeland, he wrote, would help Barack "to know where you belong."

People Listen

In his sophomore year at Occidental, Obama had his first taste of public speaking. He became involved in what was a global struggle to end apartheid in South Africa. Apartheid was a government policy of separating black South Africans from whites and of legally discriminating

Getting involved: Obama attended Occidental College in Los Angeles, California, for two years. In his sophomore year, he became part of a group of students who were protesting the apartheid system (legal, race-based discrimination) of South Africa.

IN FOCUS

Apartheid

South Africa is a country at the southern tip of Africa. During the 1800s, South Africa was a Dutch and then a British colony. The first white people in South Africa were Dutch and British settlers, who mined the area's rich deposits of diamonds and gold. In 1961 South Africa gained its independence from Britain, but the white population continued to rule. They also continued the laws of apartheid, legal separation of the races, which had been in place since 1945. Legal segregation in South Africa continued until the early 1990s, when it was outlawed and Nelson Mandela became the nation's first black president.

against them. It was similar to the Jim Crow laws once practiced in the United States. Obama spent months helping to organize a rally against apartheid. He spent a lot of time contacting prominent people and asking them to speak for the cause. During this time, he noticed something powerful. People, he realized, were interested in what he had to say. They listened to him, just as his fifth-grade classmates had listened to his father tell stories about Kenya.

On the day of the rally, Obama and some of his friends performed a skit. Obama was supposed to start giving a speech and then be carried off the stage by two white men. This was their way of showing people that apartheid kept blacks from speaking freely. The skit went as planned and got people's attention. But Obama couldn't have been more disappointed. He didn't want to be carried offstage. He wanted to continue speaking to the audience. He'd felt a connection with the crowd and a sense of belonging and purpose he hadn't felt in a long time.

A Long-Distance Call

After two years at Occidental, Obama was ready for a change. He headed to New York City to attend Columbia University. He still hadn't chosen a major, and he still longed to be part of a community. In New York, Obama started to take better care of himself. He ran 3 miles (5 kilometers) a day. And he spent a lot more time studying, something he hadn't done much of since his early days at Punahou.

In his senior year at Columbia, Obama received a long-distance phone call. He had a hard time discerning who the caller was. A woman who called herself Aunt Jane was calling from Nairobi, Kenya. Her voice was barely audible through the layer of static. Fearful that the bad connection would end the call at any time, she delivered her message quickly. She told Obama that his father had died in an automobile accident.

Columbia years: Obama poses for a photo in New York City, where he attended Columbia University. While at Columbia, he learned that his father had died in a car accident in Kenya.

Community Organizing

Barack Obama graduated from Columbia in 1983 with a degree in political science. That year he decided to become involved in community service. He wanted to make a difference. He wanted to organize communities to work for change. He knew he wouldn't make a lot of money in community organizing, but he didn't care.

He wrote to dozens of groups and communities asking if they needed an organizer. For the longest time, no one responded. Eventually he received a call from Gerald Kellman in Chicago, Illinois. Kellman had started a group called the Developing Communities Project (DCP). He was trying to get black and white communities on the South Side of Chicago to work together to save manufacturing jobs. The area was home to many steel factories that had closed down, leaving hundreds of people jobless. Kellman was white and Jewish. He needed someone the local black community would trust. Barack Obama was just that person. In 1985 Obama again packed his bags, and this time, he headed to the Midwest.

City Streets

Obama's charge was to work with church leaders. With the support of the churches, Kellman felt they could reach out for the support of the thousands of people in the community who attended those churches. Obama also needed to get to know the community. He needed to spend time in neighborhoods and listen to people's stories. He needed to learn what bothered them most, what they felt was unfair, what they feared, and what they were most concerned about. He needed to learn what causes would get people to work together for change. His job was to get to the "centers of people's lives"—to become part of the community.

Working for change was harder than Obama thought it would be. His early efforts did not yield many results. Only thirteen people showed up at the first meeting he organized. Many church leaders didn't want to work with one another, much less with Obama or Kellman. Many people in the community had been living in poverty for so long they didn't believe that change was possible. Still others did not want to put pressure on the city because they didn't want the mayor to look bad. Mayor Harold Washington was the first African American mayor of Chicago. Many blacks in the community saw him as a hero. For the first time, the African American communities in Chicago felt that perhaps the city government would help them. Many people hung his picture on their walls—in ice cream parlors, barbershops, kitchens, and living rooms.

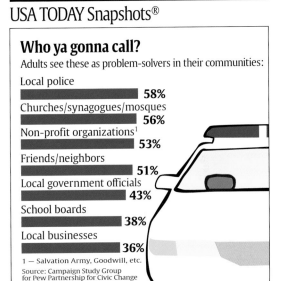

USA TODAY Snapshots®

Who ya gonna call?

Adults see these as problem-solvers in their communities:

Local police
58%
Churches/synagogues/mosques
56%
Non-profit organizations[1]
53%
Friends/neighbors
51%
Local government officials
43%
School boards
38%
Local businesses
36%

1 — Salvation Army, Goodwill, etc.
Source: Campaign Study Group
for Pew Partnership for Civic Change

By Cindy Hall and Adrienne Lewis, USA TODAY, 2001

Altgeld Gardens

Obama spent much of his time in Chicago working with the people who lived in and near Altgeld Gardens. Often referred to by residents as the Gardens, most of the area is covered with cement and asphalt. Altgeld Gardens is a housing project on Chicago's South Side. The project, built in 1945, offers housing to people with little income. It is run by the Chicago Housing Authority (CHA).

Obama experienced many setbacks, but every now and then change would happen, and he would remember why he became involved in community organizing. One of his first successes involved Altgeld Gardens and the Mayor's Office of Education and Training (MET). MET was responsible for administering a new computerized job bank.

The Gardens

Altgeld Gardens is one of the first public housing projects ever built in the United States. The federal government constructed it in 1945 to create low-income housing for African American veterans returning home from World War II (1939–1945). Although it was located in the heart of an industrial center, the government considered it to be a model for other housing projects.

The project stretches for about 190 acres (77 hectares) and houses up to thirty-five hundred people in fifteen hundred low-rise units. It includes schools, medical facilities, and a sports center. In 1956 the Chicago Housing Authority took over Altgeld Gardens and added it to its other housing projects in Chicago. About 97 percent of Altgeld's residents are African American.

The Gardens: Children walk in front of one of the buildings in Altgeld Gardens on Chicago's South Side. Obama worked with the people who lived in and around the housing project to try to improve conditions there.

People who were out of work could log in and search for jobs online. The job bank was important to the people on the South Side of Chicago. Many of them had lost their jobs when the steel plants closed. Yet months passed without anyone at Altgeld finding work through the new system.

One day Obama picked up a brochure listing the locations of MET offices where people could use the job bank and other employment resources. He immediately saw that the nearest MET office was thirty-five blocks north of Altgeld Gardens. No offices had been set up in the poorer communities of the South Side, where they were needed most. This was an issue that drew the community together. Community members did the hard work of contacting city officials and organizing rallies. Before long, Mayor Washington agreed to open a MET office near Altgeld, and he even showed up at the office's opening ceremony. This move didn't solve all the community's unemployment problems, but it was progress. For the first time since moving to Chicago, Obama felt as if he could do the job he came to do.

 In November 1987, shortly after being elected to a second term as Chicago's mayor, Harold Washington died suddenly after a heart attack. Thousands of Chicagoans from the black community mourned the death of the man they considered a hero.

Cleaning Up

The people in Altgeld Gardens had more than unemployment to worry about. The housing needed new plumbing and heating systems. In addition, toxic waste surrounded them. The housing project is near a huge landfill as well as sewage treatment plants that fill the air with foul odors.

www.usatoday.com

News

SECTION A

November 27, 1987

Washington death starts a scramble

From the Pages of USA TODAY

Chicago Mayor Harold Washington's death has created political uncertainty in the city and left a void on the national political scene.

He died Wednesday from a heart attack at the age of 65.

Thursday, meetings were held by rival factions racing to seize power in Chicago, a city often torn by political strife.

But Don Rose, a political consultant to Washington, said: ``I think we'll be plunged back into some substantial degree of political chaos.''

Chicago mayor Harold Washington

Reaction nationally:

"A tremendously important voice has been lost on the national scene for compassion and concern for poor people," said Boston Mayor Raymond Flynn, who worked with Washington on a United States Conference of Mayors housing committee.

"His influence and work on housing issues and care for the homeless far exceeded the boundaries of Chicago."

Dr. Benjamin Hooks of the NAACP said Washington's death leaves "a significant void" in the nation's black political leadership. "The tremendous support he got in his re-election translated into national political strength." Democratic candidates knew the votes he could deliver could be a key to the nomination, said Hooks. "That force will be sorely missed."

—Kevin T. McGee and Kevin Johnson

When the CHA announced that it needed to remove asbestos from its offices, Obama's group took note. Asbestos is an insulating material found around pipes in many old buildings. It is also toxic and is known to cause lung cancer in people who are exposed to it. Altgeld Gardens was built around the same time as the CHA headquarters. It was very possible that the housing project also contained asbestos.

Obama had a plan. He and community organizers urged Altgeld residents to call and write to the CHA asking them to test Altgeld apartments for asbestos or to show proof that the apartments had been tested. The CHA ignored the requests. Obama's group informed the housing agency's director that they would be showing up at his office, with or without an appointment. Obama also sent out a press release, notifying newspapers and television stations about the meeting. When he and several people from Altgeld arrived at the CHA, the director was unavailable. Just in time, the news crews started to show up. The director's assistant had no choice but to schedule the meeting at Altgeld.

Obama's strategy had worked. A few days later, the director showed up for the meeting in Altgeld's gymnasium. A record seven hundred people attended—a far cry from the thirteen people who had showed up at Obama's first meeting. Altgeld did indeed have asbestos insulation, and the CHA paid for it to be removed.

Obama and the DCP had managed to get the government to help their community. But Obama also realized that this achievement was only the tip of the iceberg. Unemployment, crime, drugs, education, and plumbing—the community had a host of other overwhelming issues to address.

Family Lessons

After his father's death, Obama kept in touch with some of his relatives in Kenya, particularly a half sister, Auma. Though they didn't write to each other often, he and Auma held onto the hope that they would meet in person one day.

October 24, 1991

TARGET OF TOXINS?
"We're not going to put up with it"

From the Pages of
USA TODAY

Low-income minority communities are coming under scrutiny as mounting evidence suggests they're disproportionately victimized by the nation's environmental problems.

"When you look at where the polluting industries locate, they're always in the backyard of a minority community,'" says former New Mexico Gov. Toney Anaya.

Perhaps one of the most blatant cases is Chicago's Altgeld Gardens, a south-side public housing complex where "when it rains it smells like dead people,'" says Antoinette Cobbins.

On one side of the complex is a waste treatment plant. A mile [1.6 km] down the road is a hazardous waste incinerator. To the south are hazardous waste landfills; to the west, steel mills and landfills; to the east, sewage treatment facilities.

In fact, Altgeld Gardens—which has no gardens because, residents say, they'd be afraid to eat the produce—is a residential island in a sea of industrial and municipal waste.

And along with the smell, residents believe, come health problems. Rowena Robinson blames lifelong asthma—and the asthma three of her four children suffer—on the air. She thinks chemicals in the air and water caused the malignant kidney tumor that killed a fifth child.

At the heart of environmental racism, say those who've studied it, is the fact that poor, minority communities rarely have the clout or technical expertise to fight polluting industries.

[They] simply [do] not believe it would help to complain.

What's more, for neighborhoods facing other poverty-driven problems—inadequate housing and education, unemployment—environmental problems aren't a priority.

But now some minority communities are fighting back.

—Rae Tyson

Auma was a university student in Germany when she came to visit Obama for the first time. He showed her around Chicago and introduced her to his friends. She was friendly and easy to be around. She shared stories about their father and the events that happened before his death. The stories his sister told were much different from the ones Obama knew.

Auma told Obama about how their father (she called him the Old Man) had a high-paying and respectable job as an economist in Kenya's Ministry of Tourism. But the Old Man spoke out harshly against Kenya's president Jomo Kenyatta. Kenyatta fired him and forbade anyone from rehiring him. The Old Man wound up poor and homeless until years later when he was offered another job. But by this time, the Old Man had started to drink a lot. He died in a drunk driving accident.

Obama's image of his father—from stories and from his only visit when Obama was ten years old—had been crushed. How could his father, so strong, intelligent, and sure of himself, end up in such dire straits?

Time to Move On

Shortly after his sister's visit in 1987, Obama resigned from his community organizing position in Chicago. He hadn't given up on his dream of working to make positive changes, but he realized that to really make a difference, he needed to do things on a larger scale. With this in mind, he applied to several law schools. With a law degree, he knew he would be better informed and better prepared to help the community. In February 1988, Harvard Law School notified him that he had been accepted. While most of the people he worked with expected this intelligent young man to move on to bigger and better things, some of them also knew he'd be back. The bonds he'd made with the community were too strong.

USA TODAY

CHAPTER THREE

Visiting Kenya: Obama traveled to Kenya before he began classes at Harvard. Here he poses at the family homestead with (*left to right*) his step-grandmother Sarah Onyango Obama, his sister Auma Obama, and his stepmother Kezia Obama, who is holding an unidentified baby.

Kenya to Harvard

Before starting law school, Obama wanted to fulfill another important dream—visiting Kenya. He longed to see if visiting his ancestral homeland would transform him, as it had done for so many other African Americans he talked with. He wanted to experience African culture and to see the beauty and wildlife he had heard so much about. And he wanted to see Auma, to meet the rest of his Kenyan family, and to visit his father's gravesite.

Obama spent several weeks in Kenya. He learned how to speak a few words and phrases in Luo, and he learned about the ways of the country. He saw that foreigners owned many of the businesses and that the waiters in hotel restaurants ignored Kenyans. Instead they catered to foreigners, whom they assumed had money. He and his sister went on safari, where they saw gazelles, wildebeests, giraffes, elephants, lions, and hyenas. They viewed the Great Rift Valley of western Kenya and the open sky with its bright stars and visible Milky Way. He discovered the role of family and tribe in Kenyan life. By experiencing the people and places that were his father's, Obama was better able to know and understand the man.

Obama left Kenya feeling content. He was ready to start law school in the United States, but he knew he'd return to Kenya someday.

Meeting family: Obama *(back row, second from left)* met many of his family members when he visited Kenya in 1987. Here he is surrounded by members of his family including his sister Auma *(front row, far left)* and his step-grandmother Sarah Onyango Obama *(front row, second from right).*

Back to School

Harvard Law School is one of the oldest and most prestigious law schools in the nation. In 1988 approximately sixteen hundred students from all over the world were enrolled in the law program. About two hundred of those students were African American, and Barack Obama was one of them.

Obama studied hard his first year at Harvard. He was older than most of the other students. Most of them had started law school directly after graduating from college. His four-year break from school as a community organizer served him well, though. He knew why he wanted to be a lawyer, and he knew what he wanted to do with his education. This knowledge, along with self-discipline, drive, and intelligence, made him an excellent student.

Law student: Obama decided to go back to school in 1988. Here he is shown on the Harvard campus while attending law school.

Fellow Harvard alum: Michelle Robinson, shown here in the Harvard yearbook, met Obama during his internship at the law firm for which she worked in Chicago.

Love at First Sight

The summer after his first year at Harvard, Obama returned to Chicago to intern at a downtown law firm. As an intern, he would work under the direction of another lawyer. Internships give students a chance to see how their lessons from school apply to what they would do on the job. The law firm assigned Obama to work with a lawyer named Michelle Robinson. Robinson was the only African American lawyer in the firm, and she was beautiful. For Obama the attraction was immediate. The first time he saw Michelle Robinson, he knew then and there that she was the love of his life.

Robinson, by nature, was a little more skeptical. She didn't like the idea of dating someone she worked with. She thought it would look silly too, if the only two black people in the office were going out

Michelle Robinson and Barack Obama almost crossed paths earlier in life. Robinson graduated from Harvard Law School in 1988, just a few months before Obama started attending Harvard.

together. But as she saw the compassionate and caring side of Obama, she too felt the attraction. The couple started dating. When Obama's internship ended, he returned to Cambridge and continued his relationship with Michelle long-distance.

Harvard Law Review

Harvard law students can learn even more about law by researching and editing articles for the *Harvard Law Review*. The journal, or scholarly magazine, is edited by students. It features articles written by judges and other law professionals. It is one of the most respected student publications on the subject of law.

In 1990, during Obama's second year of law school, a group of about sixty student-editors elected him president of the *Harvard Law Review*. He was the first African American to receive this honor in the publication's 104-year history. The media took note. Newspapers and magazines around the nation mentioned the achievement. Obama accepted an offer from a publishing company to write a book about his life experiences. Barack Obama's name made the public spotlight for the first time, even if ever so briefly.

As president of the law journal, Obama understood his role to be, as he said, "first among

Law review: Obama was elected president of the *Harvard Law Review* while in law school. He is shown here with a copy of the publication.

News

SECTION A

February 6, 1990

Briefly

From the Pages of USA TODAY

Barack Obama, 28, of Hawaii has been elected president of the *Harvard Law Review*, the first black to hold the position. Obama is a second-year law student.

equals." In other words, he was the leader, but his job was to make final decisions after considering everyone's input. He worked hard as president of the journal, spending fifty to sixty hours a week attending meetings and reviewing articles for the magazine. On top of this work, he had to study for his law classes. He gained a reputation for working well with people who had opposing viewpoints. He listened to everybody's opinions and then made a decision others usually found hard to argue with.

Most presidents of the *Harvard Law Review* graduate and go on to work as a clerk for a judge on the U.S. Court of Appeals and then for a U.S. Supreme Court justice. Obama had the same opportunities and more. Because of his high grades and his position as president of the *Harvard Law Review*, hundreds of prestigious job offers flooded his mailbox. But he had different plans—and he knew it even then, on that cold February day he was elected president of the journal. Obama planned to return to Chicago, and he planned to do more community work.

Back to the Windy City

In 1991 Barack Obama graduated from Harvard with honors. He returned to Chicago to resume community work and to be with Michelle Robinson. At this point, the two were engaged to be married. The summer of 1991, Obama took his fiancée to meet his relatives in Kenya. His family was as warm and welcoming to her as they had been to him on his first visit. They were also impressed with Robinson's ability to learn Luo. By the time the couple left Kenya, she spoke more Luo than Obama did.

Obama also took Robinson to Hawaii, and his grandparents were also impressed with her. Gramps recognized the beauty that his grandson saw in her, and Toot appreciated her sensible nature. Obama would say later that Michelle and Toot were a lot alike. Both of them were smart, caring, and sensible.

 Chicago is sometimes called the Windy City. It sits on the western shore of Lake Michigan, the second largest of the five Great Lakes. The lake is so big it seems like an ocean. And the atmosphere above the lake creates strong winds that produce swells in the water, sometimes reaching more than 8 feet (2.5 meters) high, and breezy conditions on land.

Project Vote!

When Obama returned to Chicago, he noticed a difference. After having spent three years away from community organizing, the South Side seemed rougher and people less friendly. Neighborhoods seemed to be in greater decay. This may have been just his impression, but without the support of Mayor Washington, the black communities seemed to have suffered.

In 1992 Obama took a job as director of the Chicago chapter of Project Vote!, a national organization dedicated to encouraging minorities to register to vote. In just six months, he was able to organize a campaign that registered 150,000 people to vote. A member of Chicago's City Council marveled at Obama's leadership. He said, "It was the most efficient campaign I have seen in my 20 years in politics."

That same year, an African American woman named Carol Moseley Braun was running for U.S. senator from Illinois. Her opponents were involved in a negative ad campaign, insulting each other instead of focusing on the issues. Moseley Braun won the election, partly because

Project Vote!: Illinois lawyer Carol Moseley Braun ran for the U.S. Senate in 1992 and won. She was the first African American woman to become a U.S. senator, as well as the nation's first female senator from Illinois.

October 9, 1992

Changing character of campaigns: Voters say 'no' to negativism

From the Pages of USA TODAY

"Negative campaigning is still effective," says [Bill] Clinton pollster Stan Greenberg. "But it's harder. The possibility of a backfire is greater."

Evidence can be found not only in the presidential race, in which Clinton last spring found his popularity dropped as he attacked his Democratic rivals, but in state races.

Carol Moseley Braun's victory in the Illinois Senate Democratic primary and Russ Feingold's upset in Wisconsin's Democratic Senate primary were at least partly a by-product of two other candidates tearing each other up.

—Adam Nagourney

she chose not to participate in negative campaigning but also because of Obama's efforts to increase voter registration. In 1992 Carol Moseley Braun became the first black woman ever elected to the U.S. Senate.

Marriage

Barack Obama and Michelle Robinson were married in Chicago in October 1992. Auma and other Kenyan relatives were present. Some of Barack's friends from Hawaii and from his community organizing days were also there. His mother, sister Maya, and grandmother made it to Chicago for the event, but his grandfather had recently passed away. Robinson's brother, Craig; her mother, Marian; and her extended family all came to celebrate. But her father, Frasier, died just months before the wedding.

The Reverend Jeremiah Wright Jr. presided over the wedding ceremony at Chicago's Trinity United Church of Christ, a church Obama first attended during his community organizing days. Being married to Michelle and surrounded by loving family and friends, Obama felt like the "luckiest man alive."

Big day: Michelle Robinson and Barack Obama married in Chicago on October 3, 1992.

Home sweet home: Barack and Michelle Obama bought a townhouse in this building in the Hyde Park neighborhood of Chicago in 1993. They lived here until 2005.

A Career in Politics

■■■■

The Obamas had settled into a town house in a classy section of Hyde Park, a neighborhood on the South Side of Chicago. Michelle Obama still worked for the law firm where she and her husband had met. He continued to do community work and was also busy writing the book about his life experiences.

In 1993 Obama took a job with Miner, Barnhill and Galland, a Chicago law firm that specializes in civil rights cases. He didn't make a lot of money working for the firm, but he took the job in part so he could help right some of the wrongs in society. He worked on cases where people's basic rights—their civil rights—were being violated. He again took up the cause of voting rights, in addition to discrimination cases involving employment and housing.

Teacher

At this time, Obama also started teaching constitutional law at the University of Chicago. He enjoyed teaching these classes because of all the tough questions students asked. They forced him to argue both sides of an issue.

Obama had always been fascinated with U.S. history. He marveled at the documents that the Founding Fathers, the country's early leaders, drafted. Referring to the U.S. Constitution and its Bill of Rights (the first ten amendments to the Constitution) and to the Federalist Papers, written to promote passage of the Constitution, Obama would later

Teaching moment: Obama started teaching constitutional law at the University of Chicago in 1993.

All Other Persons

Slavery had existed in colonial America for 168 years when the Founding Fathers drafted the U.S. Constitution in 1787. At the time the Constitution, the nation's body of laws, was being written, the northern states no longer relied on slave labor. The North had more industry, which didn't require the work of slaves to succeed. The southern states, whose economy was dependent on growing tobacco and cotton crops, argued that they needed a slave labor force in order to make a profit. The subject of slavery came up often during meetings of the Constitutional Convention of 1787, where lawmakers were creating a constitution for the country. If a constitution outlawed slavery, a few southern states threatened to leave the Union.

Because of these issues, the word *slavery* was not used in the original document. But the phrase "all other persons" refers to those who were not free citizens. In the Constitution, "all other persons" were counted as three-fifths of a person for the purposes of taxation and representation.

The U.S. Constitution did not have any reference to slavery until 1865. That year, lawmakers added the Thirteenth Amendment, which made slavery illegal.

write, "As we read these documents, they seem so incredibly right that it's easy to believe they are the result of natural law if not divine inspiration."

Dreams from My Father

The year 1995 was filled with many ups and downs for Obama. After five years, Obama's first book was published. In the book, called *Dreams from My Father*, he writes honestly about growing up in a white household with an absent black father. He describes his need to belong to a black community. And he examines what motivated him to want to make a difference in the world. He describes his years as

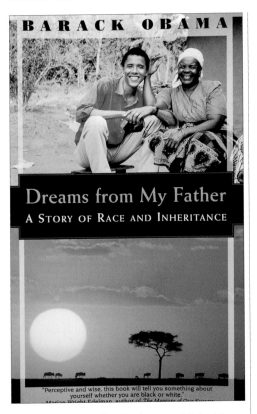

BARACK OBAMA

Dreams from My Father
A STORY OF RACE AND INHERITANCE

"Perceptive and wise, this book will tell you something about
yourself whether you are black or white."
Marian Wright Edelman, author of *The Measure of Our Success*

Author: Obama's first book was published in 1995. *Dreams from My Father* included stories from Obama's childhood in Hawaii and Indonesia, as well as his trip to Kenya.

a community organizer and gives a vivid portrayal of his time in Kenya. That same year, his mother died of cancer at the age of fifty-two. Obama would later write that she was "the kindest, most generous spirit I have ever known, and that what is best in me I owe to her."

Obama was thirty-four years old. His list of achievements had grown fast and long. Yet he was feeling restless, as if he needed to do something more. He had been mulling over the idea of getting into politics. If he were in office, he thought, he could

Abraham Lincoln is the U.S. president Obama most admires. Before being elected president in 1861, Lincoln served as an Illinois state legislator for eight years. He helped to guide the nation through the Civil War (1861–1865) before being assassinated in 1865. His leadership helped to end slavery in the United States in 1865.

Working for a Cause

Shortly after they were married, Michelle Obama quit her high-paying job at the law firm to work in public service. She worked in the office of Chicago's mayor, Richard M. Daley, before becoming executive director of the Chicago office of Public Allies.

Public Allies helps young people find jobs in public service. Later, she took a job directing community affairs for the University of Chicago Hospitals. Michelle Obama could have taken jobs that paid a lot more money. Instead, she opted to work for causes she believed in.

help more people. He wanted to improve the world. Community service was too small scale, and working through the court system was sometimes too slow. Obama knew he needed another way.

Alice Palmer

Because of his work as a lawyer and community organizer, Obama knew Alice Palmer. Palmer was a state senator in Illinois who represented the Thirteenth District. The Thirteenth District includes a large portion of the South Side of Chicago. Chicago proper is a large city of nearly three million people, and neighborhoods can change from poor to rich within a matter of blocks. The Thirteenth District is no different. Some areas are poor, others are working class, and still others are wealthy. The Thirteenth District is mostly black and Democratic.

Alice Palmer had served as state senator for four years when she announced in 1995 that she planned to run for the U.S. House of Representatives. In Congress she could serve a larger section of Illinois. Running for Congress is the next logical step for a state senator, and it made sense for Palmer. She was well liked in her district. Mel Reynolds, the current representative, was on trial and faced several criminal charges. Even if he were acquitted, it was unlikely he'd be reelected. His reputation had already damaged his chances of winning.

Palmer's decision to run for Congress proved to be an opportunity for Obama. Palmer appreciated Obama's beliefs, his intelligence and manner, and his ability to move people into action. When she announced she was going to step down from her state senate seat to run for Congress, she confidently suggested that the young and charismatic Barack Obama take her place. After careful consideration, Obama accepted the challenge. In July 1995, he began campaigning. The Democratic primary was just nine months away. He would likely have to run against some other well-known Democratic contenders. Obama got to work.

Lucky Thirteen

Shortly after Palmer announced she would run against Mel Reynolds in the 1996 election, Reynolds resigned. The court had convicted him on several criminal charges, and he would have to spend up to five years in prison. The state did not want to wait an entire year before filling the seat, so they scheduled the election to take place in two months. Because Reynolds resigned, Palmer found herself facing several other candidates who had decided to join the race. She and the other candidates had to work fast if they were going to get voter support.

Palmer lost the election to Jesse Jackson Jr., son of the famous civil rights activist the Reverend Jesse Jackson.

Family ties: Jesse Jackson Jr. *(left)* campaigns for U.S. Congress in 1995. (His father, the Reverend Jesse Jackson, is behind him.) Jackson Jr. beat Alice Palmer in the Democratic primary and went on to win the House seat.

November 28, 1995

Jesse Jackson Jr. is on today's ballot in Chicago

<u>From the Pages of</u>
<u>USA TODAY</u>

In Chicago he's known as "Junior"—as in Jesse Jackson Jr. But today the son of the two-time presidential candidate and civil rights leader is asking voters to make him Congressman Jackson.

In his first bid for elective office, Jackson, 30, faces three Democratic state legislators. All are older and more politically experienced than he. They have accused him of trading on his father's name in a bid to replace former representative Mel Reynolds, who resigned last month.

The general election is Dec. 12, but today's Democratic primary is tantamount to election in a district so Democratic that President Clinton won 80% of its votes in 1992.

The latest *Chicago Tribune* poll conducted two weeks ago showed Jackson leading state Senate Minority Leader Emil Jones, 33% to 20%. Thirty-five percent were undecided.

Jackson has been a Democratic national committeeman for seven years and worked in congressional campaigns. He has a law degree and a master's in theology, and he has been field director of the Rainbow Coalition, his father's political organization.

But Jones, 60, a 22-year veteran of the Illinois Legislature, says, "If he was Jesse Smith, he wouldn't even be a blip on the screen." Jones is endorsed by the party's ward and township leaders, which could be a key factor if voter turnout is as low as officials predict: below 20%.

Also running: state Sen. Alice Palmer, 56, who has attacked Jones' ties to Chicago Mayor Richard Daley; and state Rep. Monique Davis, 59, who says she is endorsed by former representative Gus Savage and Nation of Islam leader Louis Farrakhan.

The district, where about two-thirds of voters are black, stretches from the south side of Chicago to more affluent suburbs.

—Bob Minzesheimer

She returned to Obama, asking him to step out of the race for state senator. She had decided to run for the office again, even though she had told Obama she would retire if she lost. Obama refused. He had already started campaigning. And he wanted to get involved in politics.

Palmer decided to run anyway. She quickly gathered the signatures needed for her petition to enter the state congressional race. Obama was amazed at how fast she and the other contenders were able to get these necessary signatures. He requested a review of the petitions—for Palmer and the other Democratic candidates. Some of the signatures weren't signatures at all but printed names. And it appeared that some of the names did not belong to registered voters. The election board dismissed Palmer's petition and those of all the other Democratic candidates except for Obama, whose signatures were in order. The deadline to enter the race had passed. It was too late for other Democrats to petition to run in the Democratic primary against him.

During the Democratic primary in March 1996, Barack Obama was the only name on the ballot. In November 1996, he defeated the Republican candidate, who did not have much of a chance in the mostly Democratic Thirteenth District.

Life of a Senator

Being a state senator occupied a great deal of Obama's time. During the legislative session, he would have to take a three-hour train ride from Chicago to Springfield,

USA TODAY Snapshots®

Time it takes to get to work
Amount of time spent commuting
(in minutes)

15-29
36.1%

0-14
29.4%

45 or more
15.4%

30-44
19.1%

Source: Census 2000   By Shannon Reilly and Karl Gelles, USA TODAY, 2004

the capital of Illinois, so he could be present to cast his votes. He spent many hours drafting and presenting legislative bills, talking to the people he represented, and studying the issues. And as a first-time senator, he had to try to get to know the other state senators.

During his time in office, Obama earned a reputation for listening intently to both sides of an argument, just as he had done as president of the *Harvard Law Review*. His ability to work with Democrats and Republicans showed others that he was a reasonable person, capable of compromise and of getting things done.

In 1998, on Independence Day, Michelle Obama gave birth to a daughter. The parents named her Malia. The Obamas were attentive parents. Michelle Obama began working part-time at the University of Chicago Hospitals so she could spend more time with Malia. Obama cherished his family, and once again, he had reason to feel like the luckiest man on Earth.

A Miscalculation

Obama's lucky streak came to a temporary halt in 1999. He was restless again. He knew he wanted to accomplish things on an even greater scale. In Washington, D.C., he thought, he could help even more people. He decided to run for the U.S. House of Representatives against the incumbent (current officeholder) Bobby Rush.

His wife didn't like the idea. Neither did his friends in the state senate. Michelle Obama supported her husband's ambitions, but only to a point. She had a career of her own, and the two of them had a daughter to raise. When campaigning for office, Obama was home late and gone early or gone for days in a row. Malia was only an infant when Obama decided to run for national office. His wife wanted him to fulfill his duty as a father. She had no intention of shouldering the duties of parenthood by herself.

Obama ran anyway and was sorely defeated in the primary. Rush had a good reputation among voters. He hadn't accomplished much, but he also hadn't done anything wrong, as one voter put it.

www.usatoday.com

USA TODAY

News

SECTION A

March 22, 2000

Rep. Rush beats back challengers

<u>From the Pages of</u>
<u>USA TODAY</u>

Rep. Bobby Rush turned back a challenge Tuesday by fellow Democrats to virtually assure himself a fifth term in Congress representing the city's South Side.

Rush had been seen as vulnerable after being swamped in the mayoral election last year by Mayor Richard Daley. With nearly all of the vote counted Tuesday, however, Rush prevailed 55% to 40% over state Sen. Barack Obama, a respected local legislator and the first black editor of the *Harvard Law Review*.

—Debbie Howlett

First campaign loss: Michelle Obama and Malia watch as Obama gives a concession speech in 2000 after losing in the Illinois Democratic primary for a seat in the U.S. House.

After all the hard work and effort of campaigning, losing candidates almost always feel disappointed. Obama was no exception. He returned to Springfield a humbled man. He poured his attention into his work as a legislator, pushing for expanded health-care coverage and tax credits for the poor. In June 2001, the Obamas had their second child—Natasha, affectionately known as Sasha. Balancing family and careers became an even bigger issue than before, but the family managed.

9/11

Just a few months later, on September 11, 2001, a group of terrorists attacked the United States by hijacking commercial aircraft and flying them into buildings in New York and Washington, D.C. The terrorists destroyed the Twin Towers of New York's World Trade Center complex, killing thousands of people. A portion of the Pentagon, headquarters of the U.S. military near Washington, D.C., was heavily damaged. The world watched in horror as the United States, the most powerful nation in the world, fell victim to terrorism. The nation soon learned that the terrorists were from an Islamist militant group called al-Qaeda.

As the country worked to recover from the tragedy and to capture the terrorists, some Americans viewed Arabs living in the United States with suspicion. In 2003 the United States entered into a war against the Arab

USA TODAY Snapshots®

The cost of terrorism

U.S. insurance payouts from the terrorist attacks will be second only to the long-term costs of asbestos liability:

(in billions)

Asbestos liability	$55-$65
Sept. 11 terror attacks	$30-$58[1]
Environmental liability	$30-$40
Hurricane Andrew	$20

1 – Estimate.
Source: Tillinghast-Towers Perrin, CFO magazine

By Darryl Haralson and Frank Pompa, USA TODAY, 2002

www.usatoday.com

USA TODAY

News

SECTION A

September 12, 2001

"Act of war" decimated landmarks, killed thousands of people and stole nation's sense of security

<u>From the Pages of USA TODAY</u> Cascading terrorist attacks hit high-profile targets in New York City and Washington Tuesday, killing thousands and bringing the mad world of suicide bombers and Middle East terror home to the American mainland.

Damage from the unprecedented attack was still being tallied today, but seemed certain to include thousands of lives, millions of dollars worth of property and the nation's sense of security from the perils of a hating world.

"The pictures of airplanes flying into buildings, fires burning, huge structures collapsing have filled us with disbelief, terrible sadness and a quiet, unyielding anger," President Bush said in a 5-minute address.

"These acts of mass murder were intended to frighten our nation into chaos and retreat, but they have failed. Our country is strong. Terrorist acts can shake the foundation of our biggest buildings, but they cannot touch the foundation of America," Bush said in his televised address.

—Richard Willing and Jim Drinkard

nation of Iraq. President George Bush accused Saddam Hussein, Iraq's leader, of aiding terrorists, among other things. Initially, most Americans were in favor of the war. President Bush declared it a war on terrorism, and most people believed it would end quickly. It was in this environment that Barack Hussein Obama decided to run for the office of U.S. senator for Illinois.

Campaign prep: Obama works on paperwork in his campaign office before a televised debate with other Illinois candidates running for the Democratic nomination for U.S. Senate in 2004.

In the Spotlight

If Obama had wanted to, he could have come up with a lot of reasons not to run for U.S. senator. Barack Hussein Obama is an African name, but it sounded very similar to Osama bin Laden, the head of the al-Qaeda terrorist network. Bin Laden's name was in the news daily, as government forces tried to hunt down the terrorist who had organized the attacks on U.S. soil. Besides this handicap, Obama would have to run against six other talented candidates in the primary.

But Obama didn't care. He was driven once again by restlessness. He needed to be doing more to help his country. He wanted to win. He was confident in his abilities as a politician. And he was prepared to work as hard as necessary to reach his goal.

Obama did all the usual campaigning. He knocked on doors, passed out flyers, and held meetings. He also toured the state to talk to voters. From these conversations, he learned that most people had simple expectations and that the expectations were basically the same. It didn't matter with whom he talked, where they lived, how much money they made, or what color their skin was. People expected a job, affordable health care, high-quality education, a government they could count on, and safe streets to walk down.

A Comedy of Errors

Obama's campaign was riddled with mishaps. He would call press conferences, and no one would show up. He would enter a parade

Shaking hands: Barack and Michelle Obama shake hands with supporters after a parade on Chicago's South Side during his Senate campaign in 2004.

and be placed at the very end, waving only to the few parade-watchers still left on the streets. But he refused to become discouraged, and he kept a positive outlook. In his mind, he had no choice. Politics, he knew, was his calling.

Just weeks before the primary, Obama met with some good luck. One of the leading candidates withdrew from the race after being accused of domestic violence (violence against a family member). Obama then received the support of both of Chicago's major newspapers. In the primary on March 16, 2004, he received 52 percent of the vote, a healthy majority.

Obama needed to prepare for the next leg of the race. In November he would have to run against the Republican candidate Jack Ryan. But by June, Ryan had withdrawn from the race because of events in his personal life. Less than five months away from the election, the Republicans were without a candidate.

Democratic National Convention

Nothing did more to launch Obama into the national spotlight than the 2004 Democratic National Convention in Boston, Massachusetts. That July, Barack Obama was still a little-known state senator from Illinois who was running for U.S. senator. Most people from the Thirteenth District of Illinois knew his name, but most voters in the other forty-nine states had never heard of him. After his riveting speech at the convention, in which he spoke to the nation "not as a black American, but as an American," Obama became a star of the Democratic Party.

Obama's main message was that Americans have a lot in common. It's time, he said, to focus on what people have in common rather than on what separates them, whether race, politics, or background. He talked about his family history and of being the product of dozens of opposing influences—black, white, Asian, Muslim, Christian, and agnostic. And the audience, it seemed, could see a little bit of themselves in him.

July 29, 2004

Address throws Obama into whirlwind of political hopes

<u>From the Pages of</u>
<u>USA TODAY</u>

Barack Obama, an obscure Senate candidate from Illinois who became the Democratic Party's overnight star, was greeted Wednesday by powerbrokers and autograph-seekers talking about his future.

Even sales of his 1995 memoir, *Dreams From My Father,* soared by Wednesday morning to put him on Barnes & Noble.com's Hourly Top 100. "I still haven't had a chance to catch my breath," Obama said as he headed into a labor union reception held at the Massachusetts Statehouse.

Obama electrified the audience at the Democratic National Convention on Tuesday night with the unifying message of his keynote address and his life story as the son of a Kenyan immigrant and a woman from Kansas. The Illinois state senator is now favored to win the U.S. Senate seat.

"I think he could be our first black president," said Marsha DeFazio, 55, a Pennsylvania delegate from Pittsburgh.

His picture was on the front pages of most newspapers, and he was quickly recognized on the streets of Boston. MSNBC's Chris Matthews called Obama "a keynoter like I have never heard."

Ruth Werksman, a convention volunteer who gave her age as "late 70s," rushed up to Obama in front of the Four Seasons Hotel, kissed him and asked for his autograph. He obliged.

"You were fabulous," she said. "You spoke not as a black American, but as an American. That's what this nation is all about."

Obama says he is "flattered" by the response to his speech and that he was "proud to be one of the voices trying to make the case for the election of John Kerry and John Edwards."

When told that people were already mentioning him as a future president, Obama winced and gave a dismissive "aww" with a wave of his hand.

"I'm a state senator who hasn't been elected to higher office yet," he said. "Hopefully, I can go back to Illinois and close the deal in the next three months."

—Richard Benedetto

Keynote speaker: Obama delivered the keynote speech at the Democratic National Convention in Boston, Massachusetts, in July 2004. John Kerry, the Democratic nominee for president, had invited him to speak.

Obama's seventeen-minute speech captivated the audience of five thousand delegates and about fifteen thousand reporters and news crews. Approximately twenty million people watched the Democratic National Convention coverage on television. The following day, the media named Obama's speech a highlight of the convention. Immediately afterward, campaign contributions for Obama's U.S. Senate race increased, helping him to raise a staggering $14 million. People speculated that he would win the U.S. Senate seat in November. Others even suggested he could be president someday. Some reporters declared Barack to be "the luckiest politician in the entire fifty states."

To Washington, D.C.

Obama's now-famous speech at the Democratic National Convention practically assured that he would win the U.S. Senate race in Illinois. About three weeks after the convention, the Republicans selected Alan Keyes to run against Obama. Keyes was a strong conservative. He and Obama disagreed on many topics. And Keyes's campaign at times focused on making negative attacks against his opponent. But Obama refused to use the same tactics. He kept his campaign clean,

Face-off: Obama debates Alan Keyes, the Republican candidate for a U.S. Senate seat from Illinois, in October 2004.

Family victory: The family celebrated when Obama won the U.S. Senate seat in 2004. *From left to right:* Malia, Barack, Michelle, and Sasha

and voters responded. On Election Day 2004, Obama received 70 percent of the votes. He was headed to Washington, D.C.

Shortly after the election, even before he was sworn into office, reporters were asking Obama if he planned to run for president in the 2008 election. A U.S. senator's term is six years. Obama was firm. He planned to serve the full term, which would end in 2010.

 Throughout his term, Barack Obama was the only African American serving in the U.S. Senate.

November 4, 2004

Election 2004: The new senators;
Illinois: Barack Obama

From the Pages of
USA TODAY

Barack Obama likes to joke that his name has been something of a [problem for him]. "People will sometimes call me 'Yo Mama' or 'Alabama,'" he says.

Now his name will be among the most recognizable in the Senate.

Obama heads to Washington at the front of his freshman class. He overwhelmed Republican Alan Keyes in Illinois. After his eloquent keynote address at the Democratic convention, he also campaigned for John Kerry and colleagues seeking Senate seats in other states. He raised more than $1.3 million for them.

That hard work may help Obama land plum committee assignments. He has an eye on [the] Foreign Relations and Transportation [committees].

—Debbie Howlett

New senator: Obama attends an orientation session for new senators on November 15, 2004, at the U.S. Capitol in Washington, D.C.

"Like a Dip in a Cool Stream"

As a U.S. senator, Obama returned to Illinois throughout the year to host dozens of town hall meetings. He enjoyed meeting the people he served and listening to their stories. The meetings were generally relaxed and casual. Sometimes fifty people showed up and sometimes two thousand. Either way, Obama was grateful for the opportunity to connect with the people he served.

At these meetings, the senator listened, just as he had done during his campaign. He learned how government was affecting people's daily lives. The issues varied from health care to school funding, soil conservation, and human rights violations in foreign countries. After meeting with a group of people, Obama wrote that he felt refreshed. "My time with them is like a dip in a cool stream. I feel cleansed afterward, glad for the work I have chosen," he explained.

Office surroundings: Obama gives an interview in his Washington office in 2006. Photos of Martin Luther King Jr. and Abraham Lincoln adorned his office walls when he was a senator.

Successful author: Obama shakes hands with a fan at a book signing event in New Hampshire in 2006. His second book, *The Audacity of Hope,* became a best seller.

A Change of Heart

In 2006 Obama's second book was published. Called *The Audacity of Hope: Thoughts on Reclaiming the American Dream*, the book quickly became a best seller. People had not forgotten the keynote speaker of the 2004 convention. They wanted to know more about him and his beliefs. In the book, he calls for better politics. He argues for an end to the petty bickering between Republicans and Democrats that keeps important laws from getting passed.

"The Audacity of Hope" was the name of a sermon the Reverend Jeremiah Wright Jr. gave in 1987. It was the first sermon Obama heard in Wright's church, and it affected him deeply. *Audacity* is "an arrogant disregard for normal restraints." The sermon was a call for people to dare to be hopeful, even when everything around them has been destroyed.

By 2006, after serving two years as a U.S. senator, some people started asking Obama to run for president. In December 2006, he traveled to New Hampshire to meet with citizens in a small meeting hall, just as he had for his town hall meetings in Illinois. To his surprise, Obama was the talk of the town.

A Big Decision

The Obama family went to Hawaii over Christmas to spend time with Obama's grandmother and sister. He took this time to reflect on his future plans. By the time the Obamas returned to Illinois, he had made his decision. On February 10, 2007, Barack Obama stood on the steps of the Old State Capitol building in Springfield, Illinois, and announced that he would run for president of the United States in the 2008 election.

Big announcement: *(Left to right)* Barack, Malia, Sasha, and Michelle Obama wave to the crowd before the announcement of his candidacy for president in front of the Old State Capitol in Springfield, Illinois. In 1858 Abraham Lincoln announced his run for president from the same steps.

December 11, 2006

Obama draws crowds as he tours New Hampshire

From the Pages of USA TODAY Illinois Sen. Barack Obama surveyed the 160 journalists and 22 TV camera crews documenting his first visit Sunday to the state that holds the first presidential primary. "I am suspicious of hype," he said.

The half-Kansan, half-Kenyan author and politician, who electrified the 2004 Democratic convention with his keynote speech, says it is "a little surprising" to him and "completely baffling" to his wife that his 15 minutes of fame have extended well beyond 15 minutes.

The large crowds and pop-star response Obama drew here underscored the new reality for Democrats seeking their party's nomination: New York Sen. Hillary Rodham Clinton is no longer alone at the top.

Obama, 45, has roiled the field since he said seven weeks ago that he is weighing a run for president. He assumed the No. 2 spot among Democratic prospects in a USA TODAY/Gallup Poll last month, with 19% to 31% for Clinton. His latest book, *The Audacity of Hope*, is the No. 2 seller on Amazon.com.

"I'm still running things through the traps," Obama said Sunday when asked if he'll take the leap.

There are many signs pointing to yes. One was the trip to New Hampshire. Obama has also been contacting labor leaders and congressmen in Iowa, which holds the first caucuses. His advisers have been informally seeking recommendations for key senior positions in a national campaign.

—Jill Lawrence

On the road: Obama campaigned all across the country in 2007, including speaking at a rally in New York City attended by an estimated twenty-four thousand people.

The Campaign Trail

After announcing his candidacy in February 2007, Obama hit the campaign trail. He traveled across the country, meeting with and listening to people. He talked about the need for change, about ending the war in Iraq, and about improving the environment. He had a lot of work to do to beat the competition. In 2007 nine candidates were seeking the Democratic nomination.

He's Not Perfect

Michelle Obama was worried about her husband getting "chewed up" in politics, but she supported his dream as best she could. She believed in him, and she knew he had what it takes to become president. So she campaigned and interviewed and gave her advice. Reporters who talked to her found her to be smart, confident, and "not the least bit scripted." Michelle Obama spoke her mind. She wasn't afraid to tell reporters about her husband's flaws. She told people they couldn't expect him to be a "messiah," a savior, and that he would make mistakes like anyone else.

Supporting his dream: Michelle Obama hit the campaign trail in 2007. She campaigned for her husband in many states, including meeting with supporters in New Hampshire before that state's primary.

The Race Is On

Toward the end of 2007, polls showed the Democratic front-runners to be Hillary Clinton, John Edwards, and Barack Obama. Hillary Clinton was a senator from New York. As the wife of former president Bill Clin-

May 11, 2007

Campaigning her way

<u>From the Pages of</u>
<u>USA TODAY</u>

Spend a few minutes with Michelle Obama and it quickly becomes clear that nobody tells her what to say.

Her husband, Illinois Sen. Barack Obama, is a top contender for the Democratic presidential nomination, but in an interview with USA TODAY, she admits she hasn't thought much about what she'd do as first lady. "I survive this stuff by not getting too far ahead," she says.

Most presidential candidates and their spouses are wary of blunt talk because they fear saying something that might alienate voters or blow up into a damaging news story.

Not Michelle Obama, who says campaign advisers haven't handed her any scripts. That's apparent when she explains that she doesn't want to be "so tied to all that (Barack) is that I don't have anything for me." It's also evident as she describes the "tension and stress" in their relationship a few years ago when he was focused on his political career and she was home alone with their two kids.

Her charismatic spouse draws huge crowds, has raised as much money as New York Sen. Hillary Rodham Clinton and could become the first African-American

ton, she is also a former first lady. John Edwards is a former senator from North Carolina and 2004 vice-presidential candidate.

The Iowa caucus and the New Hampshire primary are always the first elections, and they are held in January. Whoever wins in Iowa

By Sue Kirchhoff and Greg Farrell
USA TODAY

president. Barack Obama's less famous wife, though, warns that his superstar glow will fade as voters learn more about him.

She tells USA TODAY she wants them to know that he's not the "next messiah, who's going to fix it all." She's just as direct with her audience here: "He is going to stumble . . . make mistakes and say things you don't agree with."

When she's asked what happens when her husband wants her input on policy issues, her reply isn't surprising: "Do you think I would ever hold my tongue?"

Obama, 43, says she has overcome the qualms she once had about her husband's political career and presidential ambitions. She says she's comfortable being his emissary, collecting the concerns and hopes of the voters she meets and sharing them with him. A vice president of the University of Chicago Hospitals, she now works part time and limits her campaigning to day trips so she can make breakfast for their daughters— Malia, 8, and Sasha, 5—and be home in time to tuck them in at night.

—Judy Keen

Michelle Obama

Presidential hopeful: Democratic presidential candidate Hillary Rodham Clinton, a senator from New York, campaigns in Iowa in 2007.

and New Hampshire has a good chance of being nominated at the Democratic National Convention. The race was off to a competitive start. Obama won the Iowa caucus, and Clinton came out ahead in the New Hampshire primary. By the end of January, Edwards dropped out of the race. For the first time in U.S. history, the Democratic presidential nominee would be either a woman or an African American.

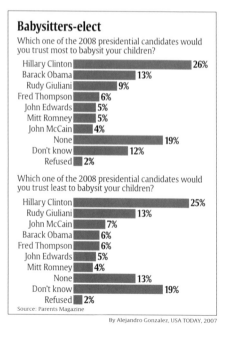

Babysitters-elect

Which one of the 2008 presidential candidates would you trust most to babysit your children?

Hillary Clinton	26%
Barack Obama	13%
Rudy Giuliani	9%
Fred Thompson	6%
John Edwards	5%
Mitt Romney	5%
John McCain	4%
None	19%
Don't know	12%
Refused	2%

Which one of the 2008 presidential candidates would you trust least to babysit your children?

Hillary Clinton	25%
Rudy Giuliani	13%
John McCain	7%
Barack Obama	6%
Fred Thompson	6%
John Edwards	5%
Mitt Romney	4%
None	13%
Don't know	19%
Refused	2%

Source: Parents Magazine

By Alejandro Gonzalez, USA TODAY, 2007

January 31, 2008

Races heat up as fields narrow

From the Pages of
USA TODAY

In an extraordinary day, [John] Edwards suspended his candidacy Wednesday where he had launched it more than a year ago.

Less than four weeks after the first votes were cast in Iowa, once-sprawling fields have been narrowed to a pair in each party with realistic chances of prevailing: New York Sen. Hillary Rodham Clinton vs. Illinois Sen. Barack Obama among the Democrats, McCain vs. former Massachusetts governor Mitt Romney [among the Republicans].

Edwards' departure apparently guarantees that the Democrats will have a breakthrough nominee: Either the first woman or first African-American to win a major-party bid for the presidency. Edwards, the Democrats' 2004 nominee for vice president, said he was stepping aside "so that history can blaze its path."

Which rival benefits isn't clear. In a USA TODAY/Gallup Poll two weeks ago, Edwards' backers split between Clinton and Obama as their second choice.

—Susan Page

Dropping out: John Edwards campaigns at a rally in Iowa in January 2007. Edwards dropped out of the race for the Democratic nomination for president at the end of January 2008, after losing the Iowa caucus and New Hampshire primary.

Parties, Primaries, Caucuses, Delegates, and Superdelegates

The Democratic Party and the Republican Party are the two largest political groups in the United States. Each party has its own set of beliefs about how to run the government. A politician usually belongs to one of the political parties. A politician can be a Democrat, a Republican, or can belong to another group, such as the Independence Party or the Green Party. Many voters also belong to a particular party.

A presidential election is held every four years on the first Tuesday in November—Election Day.

About two years before Election Day, dozens of Democrats and Republicans (and people from other smaller parties) announce that they want to run for office. In most cases, only one candidate from each party gets to be on the Election Day ballot.

Months before Election Day, all the candidates will campaign, or try to persuade voters that they are the best person for the job. Some politicians will drop out of the race within a few months, either because they run out of money or because they do not have enough public support. The rest of the candidates continue to campaign at least until the prima-

Standing tall: In 2008 Obama campaigns in Iowa, which has the first caucus in the nation.

ries and caucuses begin.

Primaries and caucuses are early elections that the major parties hold in select states. Primaries and caucuses take place early in an election year, or about eight to ten months before Election Day. In these early elections, citizens vote for one of the candidates running in their party. The number of votes a candidate gets determines how many delegates to the national convention he or she is awarded.

Delegates attend their political party's national convention, usually held two to four months before Election Day. At the convention, delegates pledge to vote for the nomination of their candidate. If a candidate who has delegates drops out of the race before the national convention, that candidate can support one of the remaining candidates.

In the 2008 Iowa caucus, for instance, voters could choose among Obama, Clinton, Edwards, and others. Obama received the most votes in Iowa and the most number of delegates. Edwards came in second, so he had fewer delegates. Clinton came in third with even fewer delegates. Edwards dropped out of the race in January 2008, before the Democratic National Convention in August. He decided to support Obama. The Iowa delegates attended the Democratic National Convention to vote for their candidate. John Edwards's delegates could vote for Edwards (even though he was no longer in the race). Or they could vote for Obama, to support Edwards's wishes, or they could vote for Clinton.

Superdelegate is a term to describe Democratic delegates who do not have to pledge their vote to a particular candidate. They are free to vote for whichever candidate they choose. Superdelegates are usually party leaders or elected officials.

At a party's national convention, the candidate who receives the most delegate votes is nominated to run against the candidate who receives the most delegate votes in the opposing party. Voters in November then choose between the two.

Caucus voter: Iowa residents vote in a caucus, held in January. Some states use the caucus voting system, while others use primaries to determine who should be a party's candidate.

Fund-Raising

Part of a candidate's job is to raise money to pay for campaign expenses, including food, hotel rooms, and airline tickets for dozens of campaign staffers. The campaign also pays for promotional materials—such as signs, buttons, and posters. The more money candidates have, the more they can spend on advertising. A short television ad can cost thousands of dollars. Unless candidates are extremely wealthy, they spend a good deal of time calling people and businesses for donations.

Most candidates hope to get most of their money from a few wealthy donors. But there are legal limits to accepting large amounts of money from a person or a business. And if the candidate does get elected, big donors may expect voting favors from the politician. The donor may tell the politician how to vote when it comes to passing laws that affect the donor's business. The public frowns on this kind of behavior. But in the scramble for money, politicians repeatedly find themselves in this position.

Obama didn't particularly like the idea of being pressured to vote against his better judgment. So instead of relying on wealthy donors

Most Americans did not have access to the Internet until the 1990s. By the end of his campaign, Obama had collected more than thirteen million e-mail addresses of people who supported him for president. This list was bigger than any list ever collected by a U.S. politician. Bill Clinton (1993–2001) and George W. Bush (2001–2009) were the only two previous U.S. presidents who had used the Internet to promote their campaigns.

www.usatoday.com

News

SECTION A

February 1, 2008

Obama sets fundraising record: $32 million in one month

Campaign drew 170,000 new donors in January

From the Pages of USA TODAY

Democrat Barack Obama raised $32 million in January—easily surpassing what any other presidential candidate has ever raised in a single month at this early stage in the battle for a party nomination, campaign records show.

Obama's chief rival, Hillary Rodham Clinton, had not released her January fundraising totals as of Thursday evening.

"This is another indication of the momentum and velocity of his campaign," Anthony Corrado, a campaign-finance expert at Colby College [in Maine], said of Obama's showing. "He's not only inspiring voters, he's inspiring people to contribute."

Obama and Clinton are racing to collect as much cash as possible to compete coast-to-coast on Tuesday, when 22 states hold primaries and caucuses, and beyond.

Campaign manager David Plouffe said Obama drew 170,000 new donors last month for a total of 650,000 contributors.

Obama and Clinton have led the presidential field in fundraising. Clinton reported raising more than $118 million last year, including $10 million transferred from her Senate campaign. Obama raised nearly $104 million.

—Fredreka Schouten

to raise money for him, he tried something different. During the campaign, he used the Internet and other technology to raise funds and to communicate with voters. Supporters of Obama set up campaign offices in towns across the country. These small offices got to know the people in the community. These offices recruited volunteers to spread the word about their candidate. People interested in Obama could go to his website and click a link to hear one of his speeches on YouTube. Or they could open MySpace or Facebook to get a better idea of who Barack Obama is.

People who liked Obama's message would donate money. Sometimes they only gave five or ten dollars, but it added up. Obama collected millions of e-mail addresses and cell phone numbers of people who visited his website. He routinely e-mailed and text-messaged his supporters, keeping them

Working the phones: Obama makes a phone call to a voter while visiting a campaign office in Kansas in October 2008.

informed of his thoughts, plans, and beliefs. Through e-mail and text messaging, Obama could quickly round up supporters to volunteer at upcoming events in their town.

By the end of his campaign, Obama had raised $660 million in contributions—more than any other presidential candidate. And he did it mostly by accepting small donations from millions of people across the nation.

Getting Ahead

By mid-March 2008, the primaries were over. Obama had received the most votes in most states and was awarded the most delegates. It appeared as if most of the superdelegates supported him as well. But the Dem-

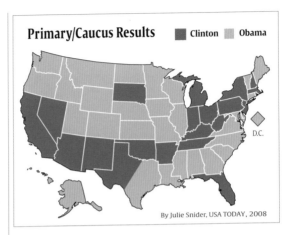

Democratic results: This map shows the breakdown of Democratic primary and caucus results in 2008.

ocratic National Convention wasn't until August. Obama knew all too well that the course of a political race can change at any time. Still, he was receiving more and more support. After John Edwards (who had twenty-six delegates to share) threw his support to Obama, other leading Democrats followed suit.

Super Tuesday: Barack and Michelle Obama celebrate with the crowd at a rally in Chicago on February 5, 2008, known as Super Tuesday. Many primaries are held across the nation on that Tuesday (the first Tuesday in February).

Different time: Obama *(left)* and the Reverend Jeremiah Wright pose together when Wright was still the pastor at Trinity United Church of Christ.

And then it happened. Tapes of the sermons of the Reverend Jeremiah Wright started showing up on the Internet and in the news. The tapes showed Wright making controversial statements about white people. Obama's link to Wright was undeniable. Wright had married the Obamas and baptized their children. By the time the media exposed Wright's comments, Wright had already retired as pastor of Trinity United Church of Christ. Otherwise, Obama said, he and his family would have left the church to worship elsewhere.

But Obama needed to do more. Instead of denying that he knew about Wright's beliefs, Obama gave a speech in Philadelphia, Pennsylvania, titled "A More Perfect Union." In his speech, Obama talked about race. He talked about what white people needed to understand about how blacks in the United States felt. He talked about how Wright had grown up when Jim Crow laws kept blacks poor and separate and how this caused blacks to mistrust the government.

He also talked about how blacks in the United States needed to understand how white people felt. Most white people and immigrants who arrived in the United States years after slavery ended do not feel connected to those wrongs. Slavery and Jim Crow laws belong to the past. And he talked about how whites and blacks basically want the same things—a job, affordable health care, a good education, and safe streets. Blacks and whites, he said, should not view themselves as enemies.

Many people appreciated what they saw as an honest look at the complexities of the racial situation in the United States. After the speech, some undecided voters decided to support Obama. Others, however, still weren't convinced that Obama would make a good president. After all, he had only served at a federal level for a few years. He had little to no foreign policy experience. The U.S. president needs to be knowledgeable about world leaders and events. The president needs to understand the sometimes complex relationship the United States has with other countries. And many people questioned how Obama would handle a terrorist attack or a major natural disaster.

Regardless of how good Obama's speeches were, many people simply did not agree with his policies. Better education and health

Warm welcome: Obama waves to a large crowd that gathered to hear him speak in Germany in July 2008. Obama spent a week traveling overseas during the campaign to meet with world leaders.

www.usatoday.com

USA TODAY

News

SECTION A

March 17, 2008

Obama's ties to minister may be 'a big problem,' some say

From the Pages of
USA TODAY Political observers debated Sunday whether Democrat Barack Obama's recently severed relationship with his controversial former minister may put the episode behind him or open new lines of attack for the presidential candidate's opponents.

The Illinois senator was dogged over the weekend about comments made by Jeremiah Wright, the former pastor of a Chicago church who has demonized white people and said the United States brought the 2001 terrorism attacks on itself.

Sen. Chris Dodd, D-Conn., who is backing Obama, said on *Fox News Sunday* that Obama's denouncing of Wright should end the matter politically. "Guilt by association is not typically American. . . . People would like to move on to other things," Dodd said.

Conservatives disagreed. They said Obama waited too long to distance himself from Wright and the matter will be raised by his Democratic opponent, Sen. Hillary Rodham Clinton, or by Republicans should he win the nomination.

"This is a huge story because it contradicts the whole persona and appeal of Obama as a man who transcends race," columnist Charles Krauthammer said. "I think it ought to be explored a lot more deeply."

Wright, former head of Trinity United Church of Christ of Chicago, has said that blacks should say "God damn America as long as she tries to act like she is God and

care translate into "big government." The government was already in debt. Why should the government continue to spend money it didn't have? Helping people can make them more dependent on the government. This can give the government too much control over the everyday lives of citizens. Many voters felt Obama's policies would harm, rather than help, the country.

supreme." He referred to America as a "country and a culture controlled by rich white people" in which the U.S. government invented HIV [the virus that causes AIDS] to kill off blacks.

On Saturday, Obama denounced Wright's comments and said "I completely reject" them.

Critics say Obama may not have ended the controversy because he has had a relationship with Wright for nearly two decades. Obama had described Wright as his spiritual mentor. He was married in the church, and Wright was a member of Obama's African American Religious Leadership Committee.

"This is a man who he chose to be associated with. It's not a family member," said Juan Williams, a Fox News analyst and National Public Radio correspondent.

He said Obama's relationship with Wright "speaks to his character, and it speaks to the judgment which is the basis on which Barack Obama has been running."

There were hints the controversy may be taking a toll on Obama's candidacy and prospects against presumptive Republican presidential nominee Sen. John McCain.

Pollster Scott Rasmussen's tracking polls of the presidential race showed McCain had moved from a tie with Obama nationally, 44%–44%, on Thursday, to a 47%–43% lead on Sunday.

According to CNN, Wright argued that Clinton's road to the White House is easier because of her skin color: "Hillary has never had her people defined as a non-person." He also said in an interview that "racism is how this country was founded and how this country is still run."

McCain has had a run-in with controversial preachers. John Hagee, the leader of San Antonio's Cornerstone Church [in Texas] accused of making disparaging remarks about Catholics, endorsed McCain. So did Rod Parsley, leader of the World Harvest Church of Columbus [Ohio] accused of urging war on Muslims.

McCain was not a member of either minister's church, and he denounced their remarks.

—William M. Welsh

Nomination

In mid-August 2008, again on the steps of the Old State Capitol building in Springfield, Obama announced his running mate. He picked Joe Biden, senior senator from Delaware. Biden had served in the U.S. Senate for twenty-six years. He also had a lot of foreign policy experience, something Obama lacked.

The 2008 Democratic National Convention was being held on August 28, 2008, in Denver, Colorado. Just a little more than four years after he first impressed the nation at the 2004 Democratic Convention, Obama appeared at the convention to give another speech. This time it was about accepting the Democratic nomination for the presidency of the United States.

Official nominee: Obama waves to the crowd at Invesco Field in Denver, Colorado, after giving his acceptance speech at the end of the Democratic National Convention on August 28, 2008.

The Republicans

Obama was the Democratic nominee, but he still had to run against candidates from other parties. The Republicans had nominated John McCain, U.S. senator from Arizona. His running mate was Sarah Palin, governor of Alaska. McCain and Palin supported many of the policies

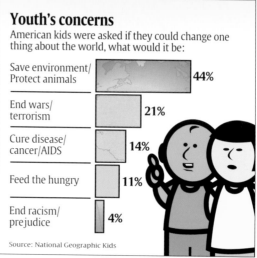

USA TODAY Snapshots®

Youth's concerns

American kids were asked if they could change one thing about the world, what would it be:

Save environment/ Protect animals — **44%**

End wars/ terrorism — **21%**

Cure disease/ cancer/AIDS — **14%**

Feed the hungry — **11%**

End racism/ prejudice — **4%**

Source: National Geographic Kids

By David Stuckey and Keith Simmons, USA TODAY, 2008

Republican ticket: Presidential candidate Senator John McCain of Arizona and vice-presidental candidate Sarah Palin, governor of Alaska, are shown at the Republican National Convention in 2008.

of the administration of President George W. Bush.

McCain and Obama differed on many issues. They debated about taxes, gun control, health care, the environment, and the war in Iraq. But as the election grew nearer, the economy became an important concern. People all across the country were losing their homes, unable to afford the monthly payments on their mort-gages. Businesses were closing, and people were losing jobs. And still U.S. soldiers were serving in Iraq, a war that had become increasingly unpopular.

As Election Day approached, polls showed that most Americans had grown weary of the leadership of George W. Bush and the Republicans. The people were ready for change, and that's exactly what Obama had been promising.

Election Day
At eight in the morning on November 4, 2008, Barack and Michelle Obama went to the polls together to cast their votes. Obama joked

Shortly before midnight on November 2, 2008, Obama received word that his grandmother Toot had died of cancer. She was eighty-six years old. This was a great loss for him. He attended a memorial service for her a few weeks later.

that his wife took so long to fill out the ballot that he had to double-check to see who she voted for. After voting Obama headed to Indiana to answer voter phone calls, and his wife dropped the girls off at school.

How the states voted
As of 2:10 a.m. ET today

■ **McCain** ■ **Obama** ☐ **Undecided**

R.I.
Del.
D.C.

Source: The Associated Press   By Julie Snider, USA TODAY, 2008

Going into the election, the polls favored Obama. It was also clear that to win, McCain needed the electoral votes from Pennsylvania and Ohio. By seven-thirty P.M. eastern time Tuesday night, the polls in Ohio had closed. Barack had won Ohio's twenty electoral votes. Later in the evening, Obama won Pennsylvania's twenty-one electoral votes. As early as eight-thirty P.M. eastern time, analysts were calling the election: Barack Obama would be the next president of the United States.

When all the poll results were calculated, Barack Obama had 365 electoral votes to John McCain's 173 electoral votes. Electoral votes are cast by electors from each state. Electors are people who formally

The 1800s saw the nation's highest voter turnout, usually at around 75 percent. An estimated 66 percent of eligible voters turned out for the 1908 presidential election, when Republican William Howard Taft defeated Democrat William Jennings Bryan.

elect the president and vice-president. A state's population determines how many electoral votes it gets. To win the election, a candidate needs a minimum of 270 electoral votes. Slightly more than 64 percent of eligible voters cast their ballots that day. Voter turnout was the highest it had been in one hundred years. Young voters, African Americans, and older adults who had never before registered to vote turned out in record numbers.

Yes We Can!

On a windy stage in downtown Chicago's Grant Park, near Lake Michigan, Barack Obama and his family stood before a cheering crowd. An estimated 240,000 people had gathered to hear him speak on election night. He began by praising the United States as a country where all things are possible: "If there is anyone out there who still doubts that America is a place where all things are possible, who still wonders if the dream of our founders is alive in our time, who still questions the power of our democracy, tonight is your answer."

Obama continued, thanking his family and everyone who helped with the campaign. He talked about how the campaign started with little money and how it was built up by the five- and ten-dollar contributions of his supporters. He talked about a government by the people and for the people. The crowd cheered nonstop, crying and laughing, filled with joy and hope. They began to chant one of Obama's campaign slogans: Yes we can! Yes we can!

Victory wave: (*Left to right*) Barack and Michelle Obama and Jill and Joe Biden wave to the crowd at Grant Park in Chicago on election night.

CHAPTER SEVEN

Cabinet maker: Obama *(right)* talks with his future chief of staff Rahm Emanuel. Emanuel, a U.S. congressman from Illinois, was one of the first appointments Obama made after the election.

A New Era of Responsibility

■■■■

The ten-week gap between election and inauguration, the official swearing in of the president, gave president-elect Barack Obama time to prepare. He spent his days picking cabinet members, or people he wanted to lead various departments of the government, such as the Environmental Protection Agency and Homeland

Security. Cabinet members are important because the president turns to them for advice on issues related to their office. Each cabinet pick must be approved at a Senate hearing. For secretary of state (the head of the Department of State, which deals with international issues), Obama picked his old rival Hillary Clinton.

In addition to building his team of advisers, Obama's number one focus was on creating a plan to rescue the economy. The United States was in a full-blown recession, or a widespread decline in production, trade, and jobs. Millions of Americans were losing their jobs, their savings, and their homes.

Former rivals: Obama talks with Hillary Rodham Clinton after a press conference in December 2008 announcing her as his choice for secretary of state.

The First Lady

Michelle Obama also used this time to prepare. As first lady, she is expected to work for a special cause. She spent time thinking about ways to help military families and women who cannot earn enough money to support their families. But her number one priority was her family. She was concerned about raising Malia and Sasha in the White House. Life would be very different for the girls, who were used to their school and neighborhood. The president, vice president, and their families are guarded full-time by members of the U.S. Secret Service. As children of the president, the girls would always be followed by Secret Service agents and would get a lot of attention from reporters. This lifestyle would be anything but normal. Michelle Obama contacted former presidential candidate and former first lady Hillary Clinton for advice. She thought that the Clintons had done a good job raising their daughter, Chelsea, in the White House. She

First lady: Michelle Obama was busy before the inauguration to get everything ready for the family to move into the White House, including choosing schools for the girls to attend.

was also busy making arrangements to have her mother move to the White House too so she could be with her grandchildren.

After Obama was elected, the U.S. Secret Service immediately gave the family code names. Barack is Renegade, Michelle is Renaissance, Malia is Rosebud, and Sasha is Radiance. The media made this information public, but it didn't really matter. The code names aren't meant to be secret. They are just words that are easily pronounced and understood over radios. All presidential families get code names.

www.usatoday.com

News
SECTION A

November 5, 2008

Michelle Obama keeps her focus on her family

<u>From the Pages of USA TODAY</u>

On the day she became the next first lady, Michelle Obama worked her usual double shift: campaigner and mom.

As she has since her husband, Democrat Barack Obama, started running for president 20 months ago, Michelle Obama toggled on Tuesday between campaigning and wrangling the couple's two daughters, Malia, 10, and Sasha, 7.

She voted with her husband, greeted by reporters and a long line of voters. She took so long to fill out the paper ballot that Barack Obama joked afterward, "I had to check to see who she was voting for." Then she dropped her children at school.

Like her husband's former Democratic rival Hillary Rodham Clinton, Obama will be a first lady who is a lawyer and working mother, with degrees from Princeton and Harvard.

And, like her husband, she will break a barrier: a descendant of slaves moving into the White House as first lady.

The campaign repeatedly said she never spent more than a night away from her children, and they never missed school or a soccer game because Mom was helping Dad run for president. The last time the White House was home to children so young was when Amy Carter, 9, moved in in 1977.

Many of Obama's campaign events focused on military families and women's economic issues. Those may be her concerns as first lady, but no decisions have been made.

"She obviously has those ideas of what she'd want to work on, but as far as adjusting to the role," she hasn't looked past Election Day, Katie McCormick Lelyveld, Obama's spokeswoman, says. "She'll cross the rest of the bridges when she gets there."

—Martha T. Moore

Game Plan

During the weeks after the election and before the inauguration, Barack Obama worked hard to prepare for office. The problems facing the nation needed immediate attention. If lawmakers waited, Obama argued, the U.S. economy might not recover. His success as president would depend on how he handled the economic crisis.

Obama's belief in preparation and self-discipline served him well in his role as president-elect, when he sometimes worked day and night. He and his advisers prepared a plan to strengthen the economy. The goal of the plan was to create new jobs—and lots of them. When employed, people can buy homes, cars, and cloth-

Love of basketball: Obama's love of basketball came up many times as he prepared to take office. He also lobbied to be able to keep using his cell phone for calling and e-mailing after becoming president.

ing. When people buy products, they help keep people who make and sell these products employed. Obama's economic plan also considers the environment. Many of the jobs President Obama aims to create involve working to improve the environment.

www.usatoday.com

USA TODAY

News

SECTION A

January 9, 2009

A bold course for dire times

<u>From the Pages of</u>
<u>USA TODAY</u>

Faced with the biggest economic crisis since the Great Depression [a severe economic downturn from 1929–1942], President-elect Barack Obama already has assumed the burden of the presidency—and with it the opportunity to shape his legacy and make the economy go boom or bust.

Twelve days before taking the oath of office, Obama on Thursday urged Congress to act swiftly on his still-emerging plan to ignite the smoldering economy or risk sinking "deeper into a crisis that at some point, we may not be able to reverse."

Obama summed up the gravity of the situation in the space of 18 minutes Thursday.

"For every day we wait or point fingers or drag our feet, more Americans will lose their jobs. More families will lose their savings. More dreams will be deferred and denied," he said. "That's why I'm asking Congress to work with me and my team day and night, on weekends if necessary, to get the plan passed in the next few weeks."

When Obama places his hand on Abraham Lincoln's Bible a week from Tuesday, he will face a meltdown unlike any faced by the 11 presidents since Roosevelt: Unemployment at 6.7% and rising. A contracting economy. Plummeting home values. Nearly frozen credit markets. And a 38% drop in the Dow Jones Industrial Average since October 2007 that has sapped Americans' savings.

Lessons from history

Days before [Franklin] Roosevelt's first inauguration in 1933, George Mason University historian Richard Norton Smith says, a friend told FDR [Roosevelt] that if he ended the Great Depression, he would be remembered as one of the nation's greatest presidents. If he failed, Roosevelt replied, he might be the last president.

Hyperbole aside, historians see a similar situation today. If the economy recovers and the budget can be tamed, they say, the nation's first black president could go down as one of the greats, alongside the likes of Roosevelt and one of Obama's heroes, Lincoln, who ended the Civil War.

—Richard Wolff

Inauguration

The days leading to the inauguration were filled with excitement. Barack Obama, Joe Biden, and their families started out on a daylong whistle-stop tour. They rode an old railcar from Philadelphia, Pennsylvania, to Washington, D.C., stopping along the way in Wilmington, Delaware (Biden's home state), and Baltimore, Maryland. In each town, they greeted citizens and gave a speech. The route they took was the same one Abraham Lincoln took on his whistle-stop tour almost 150 years earlier. Once they arrived in Washington, D.C., they prepared for Inauguration Day, when Obama and Biden would be sworn into office.

USA TODAY Snapshots®

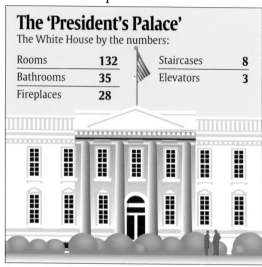

The 'President's Palace'
The White House by the numbers:

Rooms	132	Staircases	8
Bathrooms	35	Elevators	3
Fireplaces	28		

Source: The White House   By David Stuckey and Karl Gelles, USA TODAY, 2008

 Barack Obama is the forty-fourth president of the United States, but Joe Biden is the forty-seventh vice president of the United States. How could the nation have more vice presidents than presidents? Presidents reelected to serve more than one term keep the same ranking, or number, they received on their first term. But in their second term, they may have a different vice president.

The Lame Duck Amendment

From 1789 until 1937, most presidential inaugurations took place on March 4 following the November election. Early lawmakers had good reason for the delay. First, they wanted to be sure the weather had warmed up. But communication and transportation also created other issues. Before telephones, radios, and television sets, messengers delivered results from voting polls across the nation usually by horseback. It sometimes took weeks before all the results reached Washington. Once candidates knew the results, the newly elected president, vice president, and lawmakers needed plenty of time to get from their homes to Washington, D.C. In the late 1700s and early 1800s, the only way to travel was by foot or horse. Getting to Washington, D.C., could take weeks or even months.

Eventually trains and steamboats and later cars and airplanes speeded up transportation. By 1932 Congress had decided that waiting four months after the election to inaugurate the new president no longer made sense. In fact, they felt it did a fair amount of harm, prolonging what is called a lame duck session of Congress. A lame duck session refers to the period of time after a presidential election and before the newly elected president and lawmakers take office. During this time, the old Congress needs to finish old business. The shorter this time is, the sooner the new Congress can get to work.

To address the problem of a lame duck session, in 1933 Congress enacted the Twentieth Amendment to the U.S. Constitution. It states that inauguration will take place on January 20—two and a half months after Election Day. The first president sworn into office under the new law was Franklin D. Roosevelt. His second term in office officially began January 20, 1937. Because Congress added the amendment to shorten lame duck sessions, the Twentieth Amendment is often referred to as the Lame Duck Amendment.

Thumbs up: Sasha Obama gives her dad the thumbs up after he is sworn in as president of the United States. Also pictured are Michelle Obama *(top left)* and Malia *(bottom right).*

On January 20, 2009, an estimated 1.8 million people flooded a 2-mile (3.2 km) stretch of the National Mall in Washington, D.C., to witness Barack Obama's inauguration. Most of them waited for hours in the cold, hoping to catch a distant glimpse of this historic event. Obama was sworn in outside the nation's Capitol, a building constructed at the turn of the nineteenth century by slaves. He placed his right hand on a leather-covered Bible that had belonged to Abraham Lincoln and took the oath of office.

Barack's inauguration speech was powerful but somber. He talked about the common ground Americans share, a collective interest in liberty and justice. He talked about fear versus hope and the sapping of confidence across the nation. He talked about a new era of responsibility and the need for Americans to work together to meet the nation's goals. He talked as a leader—a leader for change.

His Guiding Light

Obama's presidency began during a turbulent time in American history. The financial and housing crisis, unemployment, the war in Iraq, and the ongoing issues of health care, taxes, the environment, and crime weigh on most Americans' minds. Most people in the nation are affected by at least one of these issues. As Obama learned during his early days of community organizing, where there is self-interest, there is the ability to move people into action to change things for the better.

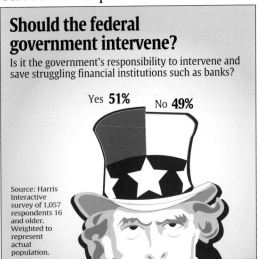

USA TODAY Snapshots®

Should the federal government intervene?

Is it the government's responsibility to intervene and save struggling financial institutions such as banks?

Yes **51%** No **49%**

Source: Harris Interactive survey of 1,057 respondents 16 and older. Weighted to represent actual population.

By Jae Yang and Veronica Salazar, USA TODAY, 2008

Barack Obama's grandmother Toot was once quoted as saying about him, "When he was a young man, I asked him what he wanted to do with his life. He said, 'I want to leave the world a better place than when I came in.' And I believe that has been his guiding light."

www.usatoday.com

News

SECTION A

January 21, 2009

Dawn of 'a new era'

From the Pages of USA TODAY

Barack Hussein Obama of Illinois assumed the full weight of the presidency Tuesday with a nod to his unique place in history, a list of economic and foreign policy problems to fix and a vow to "begin again the work of remaking America."

"The challenges we face are real. They are serious and they are many. They will not be met easily or in a short span of time," the nation's 44th president said. "But know this, America: They will be met."

Looking west from the Capitol at a record crowd of about 1.8 million people who swarmed Washington's National Mall, Obama pledged to right an economy that lost 2.6 million jobs last year and begin withdrawing U.S. troops from Iraq. Doing that, he said, would require choosing "unity of purpose over conflict and discord."

The noontime inauguration of the nation's first African-American president marked a transfer of power from the stalwart conservatism of George W. Bush to the

Inauguration crowd: More than one million people flocked to the National Mall in Washington, D.C., on Inauguration Day to see Obama sworn in as the forty-fourth president of the United States.

government activism embraced by Obama and Vice President Biden of Delaware. As the Dow Jones industrial average plunged 4% to its lowest closing in two months, Obama pledged to create jobs, rebuild roads, transform schools. "We will harness the sun and the winds and the soil to fuel our cars and run our factories," he said.

The 47-year-old son of a black man from Kenya and a white woman from Kansas spoke before a mosaic of humanity that stretched about 2 miles [3.2 km] to the Lincoln Memorial, where Martin Luther King Jr. delivered his I Have A Dream speech in 1963.

Dancing the night away: The Obamas attended ten different balls the evening of the inauguration.

Obama took the oath on the Bible of Abraham Lincoln, his hero and fellow president from Illinois, whose signing of the Emancipation Proclamation 146 years ago helped lead to this day. As first lady Michelle Obama and young daughters Malia and Sasha looked on, Obama referred to himself as "a man whose father less than 60 years ago might not have been served at a local restaurant."

The young president served notice that unlike Bush, whose war on Islamic terrorism included tactics likened to torture, "we reject as false the choice between our safety and our ideals." He offered "a new way forward" to the Muslim world "based on mutual interest and mutual respect."

Though his reflections on Bush's tenure were harsh, the passing of the torch was amicable. It began with morning coffee at the White House and ended as the ex-president boarded a helicopter that would launch his journey home to Texas.

The Obamas then walked parts of the Pennsylvania Avenue parade route from the Capitol to the White House, buildings that slaves helped erect. They watched the parade slip into darkness and attended Inaugural Balls well into the night.

Today, the hard task of governing begins. Obama plans to meet with his economic team to plot the progress of his $825 billion stimulus package, set for House action next week. He also will meet with his national security team on topics ranging from the conflict in Gaza to the Iraq troop withdrawal.

—Richard Wolff

GLOSSARY

agnostic: a person who is doubtful about the existence of God

amendment: a change in, or addition to, the Constitution

apartheid: political, economic, and legal discrimination based on the color of a person's skin

ballot: a sheet of paper used to vote

Bill of Rights: the first ten amendments of the U.S. Constitution

cabinet: a body of high-ranking members of government

campaign: to try to persuade people to vote for a politician running for a public office

candidate: a person who is trying to be elected into public office

caucus: a closed meeting of a group of persons belonging to the same political party to select candidates for the general election

civil rights: personal rights guaranteed and protected by the Constitution

Democrat: member of the Democratic Party

Democratic Party: the oldest continuously operating political party in the United States. The Democratic Party generally favors liberal, or socially progressive, policies.

Federalist Papers: a series of eighty-five essays written in 1788 by Alexander Hamilton, James Madison, and John Jay to convince voters in New York to approve the new nation's constitution

Founding Fathers: the political leaders who helped establish the United States of America

incumbent: the current holder of a political office

Jim Crow laws: laws that legalized the segregation of African Americans after the Civil War (1861–1865)

keynote speaker: a person who delivers a speech about the central fact, idea, or mood of an event

petition: a formal request submitted to a person of authority and usually containing signatures

politics: the activities and affairs involved in managing a state or government

primary: an election in which voters choose which candidate they want to represent a political party in the general election

rally: a large gathering of people intended to arouse support and enthusiasm

recession: a widespread decline in a country's production, trade, and employment lasting six months to a year

Republican: member of the Republican Party

Republican Party: one of two major political parties in the United States. Often called the Grand Old Party, or GOP, the Republican Party generally favors conservative policies.

segregation: a social system that provides separate facilities for minority groups

U.S. Constitution: a document originally written in 1787 and ratified (approved) in 1789 that is the supreme law of the United States and that provides a framework for the organization of the U.S. government

whistle-stop tour: a series of brief appearances or speeches by a politician at a number of small towns over a brief period of time and by train

Whistle-stop tour: Joe Biden *(left)* and Barack Obama wave from the train as they ride from Philadelphia, Pennsylvania, to Washington, D.C., before the inauguration in January 2009. They made many stops along the way.

SOURCES

4   Richard Benedetto, "Address Throws Obama into Whirlwind of Political Hopes," *USA Today*, July 29, 2004.

12   Barack Obama, *Dreams from My Father* (New York: Three Rivers Press, 2004), 33.

13   Ibid., 37.

13   Ibid.

15   Ibid., 48.

16   Ibid., 30.

20   Ibid., 69.

23   Ibid., 76.

23   Ibid., 91.

25   Ibid., 114.

28   Ibid., 188.

40–41   Fox Butterfield, "First Black Elected to Head Harvard's Law Review," February 6, 1990, *New York Times*, 2008, http://www.nytimes .com/1990/02/06/us/first-black-elected-to-head-harvard-s-law-review.html?scp=2&sq=obama,%20harvard%20law%20 journal&st=cse (November 14, 2008).

43   Gretchen Reynolds, "Vote of Confidence," *Chicago*, January 1993, http://www.chicagomag.com/Chicago-Magazine/ January-1993/Vote-of-Confidence/ (December 29, 2008).

45   Obama, *Dreams from My Father*, 442.

48   Barack Obama, *The Audacity of Hope: Thoughts on Reclaiming the American Dream* (New York: Vintage Books, 2006), 107.

49   Obama, *Dreams from My Father*, xii.

60   Benedetto, "Address Throws Obama into Whirlwind of Political Hopes."

63   Obama, *The Audacity of Hope*, 23.

66   Ibid., 121–122.

71   Judy Keen, "Candid and Unscripted, Campaigning Her Way," *USA Today*, May 11, 2007.

71   Mendell, *Obama*, 91.

71   Keen, "Candid and Unscripted, Campaigning Her Way."

89   "President-elect Barack Obama in Chicago," *YouTube*, November 4, 2008, http://www.youtube.com/watch?v=Jll5baCAaQU (December 5, 2008).

99   Mendell, *Obama*, 6.

SELECTED BIBLIOGRAPHY

Davis, William Michael. *Barack Obama: The Politics of Hope*. Stockton, NJ: OTTN Publishing, 2008.

Fouhy, Beth. Associated Press. "Obama to Pioneer Web Outreach as President." November 12, 2008. Available online at http://news.yahoo .com/s/ap/20081112/ap_on_el_pr/obama_network (November 12, 2008).

Mendell, David. *Obama: From Promise to Power*. New York: Amistad, 2007.

Obama, Barack. *The Audacity of Hope: Thoughts on Reclaiming the American Dream*. New York: Vintage Books, 2006.

_____. *Dreams from My Father*. New York: Three Rivers Press, 2004.

Reynolds, Gretchen. "Vote of Confidence." *Chicago*, January 1993. http:// www.chicagomag.com/Chicago-Magazine/January-1993/ Vote-of-Confidence/ (December 29, 2008).

Thomas, Evan, and Richard Wolffe. "Obama's Lincoln." *Newsweek*, November 24, 2008, 29–31.

Thomma, Steven. "Barack Obama: 44th President of the United States." *St. Paul Pioneer Press*, January 21, 2009.

Time magazine editors. "Change Has Come to America." Commemorative issue. *Time*, November 17, 2008.

Walsh, Kenneth T. "Barack Obama Elected President." *U.S. News and World Report*, November 4, 2008. http://www.usnews.com/articles/news/ campaign-2008/2008/11/04/barack-obama-elected-president.html (November 5, 2008).

FURTHER READING AND WEBSITES

Books

Arnold, James R. *The Civil War*. Minneapolis: Twenty-First Century Books, 2005.

Brill, Marlene Targ. *Michelle Obama: From Chicago's South Side to the White House*. Minneapolis: Lerner Publications Company, 2009.

Daley, James. *Great Speeches by African Americans: Frederick Douglass, Sojourner Truth, Dr. Martin Luther King, Jr., Barack Obama, and Others*. New York: Dover Publications, 2006.

Editors of *Life* Magazine. *The American Journey of Barack Obama*. New York: Little, Brown and Company, 2008.

Fremon, David K. *The Jim Crow Laws and Racism in American History*. Berkeley Heights, NJ: Enslow Publishers, 2000.

Guernsey, JoAnn Bren. *Hillary Rodham Clinton: Secretary of State*. Minneapolis: Twenty-First Century Books, 2010.

Manheimer, Ann. *Martin Luther King Jr.: Dreaming of Equality*. Minneapolis: Twenty-First Century Books, 2005.

Morris-Lipsman, Arlene. *Presidential Races: The Battle for Power in the United States*. Minneapolis: Twenty-First Century Books, 2008.

Roberts, Jeremy. *Abraham Lincoln*. Minneapolis: Twenty-First Century Books, 2004.

Thomas, Garen. *Yes We Can: A Biography of Barack Obama*. New York: Feiwel and Friends, 2008.

Websites

Barack Obama's speech at 2004 Democratic National Convention
http://www.youtube.com/watch?v=eWynt87PaJ0
A video of Obama's keynote speech is available at this site.

Barack Obama's 2004 Democratic National Convention Speech
http://www.2004dnc.com/barackobamaspeech/
This site has a transcript of Obama's keynote speech.

White House
http://www.whitehouse.gov
This website provides information about activities of the current administration.

INDEX

PHOTO ACKNOWLEDGMENTS

The images in this book are used with the permission of: © Sam Riche/USA TODAY, p. 1; © Tim Dillon/USA TODAY, pp. 3, 4, 43, 66, 94; © H. Darr Beiser/ USA TODAY, pp. 5, 6 (top), 87; AP Photo/Obama for America, pp. 7, 45, 47; © Maxine Box/Getty Images, p. 8; The Granger Collection, New York, p. 10; AP Photo/Obama Presidential Campaign, pp. 11, 17, 19, 24, 27, 40; © Co Rentmeester/Time & Life Pictures/Getty Images, p. 12; AP Photo/SDN Menting 1, HO, p. 14; © John Warburton-Lee/DanitaDelimont.com, p. 20; Punahou School Archives, pp. 18, 23; Occidental College Archives, pp. 22, 25; AP Photo/ Charles Rex Arbogast, pp. 30, 90; © Robert Deutsch/USA TODAY, 32 (top), 34, 41, 44, 52, 55 (top), 57, 61, 65 (top), 69, 72, 75 (top), 79, 84, 93, 95, 98, 100 (top); AP Photo/Charlie Knoblock, p. 32 (bottom); INS News Agency/Rex Features USA, p. 36; © Solo/INT/ZUMA Press, p. 37; © Steve Liss/Time Life Pictures/Getty Images, p. 38; 1988 Harvard Law School Yearbook/Courtesy of Special Collections Department, Harvard Law School Library , p. 39; © AFP Photo/Saul Loeb/Getty Images, p. 46; AP Photo/Seth Perlman, p. 49; © Steve Kagan/Getty Images, p. 51; AP Photo/Frank Polich, p. 55 (bottom); AP Photo/M. Spencer Greene, pp. 58, 76; © Scott Olson/Getty Images, p. 59; © Eileen Blass/USA TODAY, p. 62; © Nam Y. Huh-Pool/Getty Images, p. 63; Vandell Cobb/Ebony Collection via AP images, p. 64; AP Photo/Charles Dharapak, pp. 65 (bottom), 91; AP Photo/Jim Cole, p. 67; © Anne Ryan/USA TODAY, pp. 68, 81; © Todd Plitt/USA TODAY, p. 70; © Josh T. Reynolds/USA TODAY, pp. 71, 73; © Gannett News Service/Justin Hayworth/The Des Moines Register/USA TODAY, p. 74 (top); © David Peterson/The Register/USA TODAY, p. 75 (bottom); Rod Lamkey, Jr/ZUMA Press, p. 77; © Jack Gruber/USA TODAY, p. 80, 89; AP Photo/Trinity United Church of Christ, p. 82; AP Photo/Jae C. Hong, p. 83; © Rob Schumacher/USAT TODAY, p. 86 (top); The White House, p. 92; Evan Eile/USA TODAY, p. 100 (bottom), 101; The News Journal/Ron Soliman/USA TODAY, p. 103.

Front cover: AP Photo/Charles Dharapak; back cover © Tim Dillon/USA TODAY.

ABOUT THE AUTHOR

Karen Sirvaitis is a freelance writer and editor. She has worked mostly on nonfiction books for children and adults. She has written more than twenty books under various pen names. She lives in northwestern Wisconsin with her family.